DIVINE
DISTURBANCE
BROKEN TO BUILD

you are changing the world!
God Bless
Phillip Kelley

PHILLIP KELLEY

Divine Disturbance: *Broken to Build*

PHILLIP KELLEY

ISBN 978-0-9863262-0-2

Cover and graphic design: Michael Hildebrand
Editor: Kelli Sallman

This book is dedicated to my wife, Frances,
and our two princesses, Caroline and Madelyn.

(Caroline and Madelyn were my early morning writing buddies
sitting crisscross applesauce in our unfinished basement
next to the space heater, playing games
while their daddy typed away.)

Contents

Prologue

I set out to write this book to help people reach their God-given potential. God had different plans. I quickly realized that he wanted to overhaul my heart and change the trajectory of my life. This book was his catalyst to do just that. These are not just words on a page, but the details of a fellow pilgrim on the road to pursuing what God wants. I am a different man than when I started writing two years ago. In fact, I've had to go back and rewrite several sections because the man who initially wrote those parts hadn't experienced the Divine Disturbance yet.

God had to break me of myself. My pride. My ego. My reputation. My. My. My. He had to bring me to the place where I was actually *living* these building blocks instead of merely writing about them. Living these is painful, but necessary. Our heavenly Father's aim in the pain is never to punish, but to prune. I sit here today a broken man. And I'm extremely grateful. There is beauty in the brokenness. I pray that the shrapnel of the explosion God set off in my heart, my personal Divine Disturbance, is never removed from my soul. For these are scars of love and life.

If you want an easy read and a warm fuzzy, then do yourself the favor and put this book down. It will be better for everyone. This book is not intended for the kiddy pool. This is not a quick fix or a self help. It is more than that. It is a call to be undone. Wrecked.

Disturbed. It is a call to live your life with reckless abandon for the dream that God has for you.

If you are reading this, I have been praying for you. I am praying for you as I type, and tears are falling on my cheeks. Here's my prayer:

> *Father, I pray for the men and women who will read the following pages. I pray that you will set off an explosion in their hearts as you did in mine. I pray that they will read these words with an open mind to allow your Holy Spirit to work in them wholly. Rock them. Shake them. Disturb them. And then, Father, build them back up for great things. Give them your favor as they take this journey. In Jesus' name, Amen.*

Phillip Kelley
February 10, 2014
Overland Park, Kansas
Currently 4*

Introduction

Are you a sundial in the shade?

Read that again and focus on its imagery.

Sundials fulfill their purpose by standing in the light. Even a child can recognize the waste of a sundial in the shade.

Yet I see sundials tragically hibernating in the shade everyday— in schools, homes, businesses, and, mostly, in churches. No, I'm not going around and seeing *literal* sundials under school stairwells or tucked away behind the church baptistery. The sundials I see have names, faces, stories, and, sadly, excuses. They are the people who, at one time in their lives, had a strong calling from God. But for whatever reason, they are neglecting the potential inside of them. They were designed for a destiny (sunlight), but are withering away in complacency and comfort (shade).

What happens when you are a sundial in the shade?
- Your dreams that "once were" shrivel away and perish in the frigid, never-ending winter of self-pity.

- Your "could be" and "should be" visions die on the vine of criticism and failure.

- Your passion for making a dent in the world erodes into a passion for comfort.

- The gap between your potential and your progress creates a new San Andreas Fault—distancing you from God's best.

So, let me ask that question to you again. Are you a sundial in the shade? If so, you're in good company. **Welcome.**

The following pages reveal an Old Testament sundial named Nehemiah who emerged from the shade of his comfortable lifestyle and changed the world for his generation. This sundial had a name, face, and fascinating story. But unlike most sundials, this one lacked the list of excuses for remaining in the shade. Instead, it came with a series of building blocks—ten to be exact—that give us a place to start and a path to follow.

BUCKLE UP

This book is a *progression*. It moves. It builds. It transitions step-by-step through the Old Testament book of Nehemiah and unpacks the ten key building blocks that made this ancient bartender's dream become a reality. These building blocks are each pregnant with implication. As you pause and reflect on each one, I want to challenge you to find yourself in the story. You'll immediately recognize where you are.

When I talk about these ten building blocks with people ranging from NFL players and coaches to stay-at-home moms, everyone seems to immediately relate. These building blocks are simple. Extremely simple. But don't let their simplicity fool you. As adults, we often don't need to learn something new. We need to be reminded of what we already know. It's less about knowing and more about applying. I pray that you'll apply these

Rather than learning something new, we often merely need to be reminded of what we already know.

building blocks to the story you're writing and bring others along the way.

LET'S CHANGE THE WORLD

Let me begin with this premise: *You can change the world for your generation.* I believe this to my core. Likely, if you are reading this, you have felt the initial tugs toward such an audacious calling. However, if you're like most when hearing the challenge to change the world, you shrink back and, like a turtle playing video games in bed, retract your head into your protective shell, pound the snooze button (again), and continue living vicariously through others.

Let me say it again: You can change the world for your generation.

Enter doubt.
Open the floodgates of "I can't"
and "I'm not good enough."
Release the hounds of "not me."

That's pretty much the same response that we all have when presented with the daunting task of changing the entire existence of humanity in one fell swoop. Relax pilgrim. Take a breath.

It's normal. I've heard it said, "If the size of your dream is not intimidating to you, it's probably insulting to God." So be encouraged when you experience doubt. But don't let it take you captive. Don't be ensnared in its web. Don't let doubt become your Snuggie.

So what do we do? What do we do when our desires and dreams come face-to-face with our doubts and disappointments? Tragically, most of us *do nothing.* We sit and "pray about it." But I've known people who have "prayed" about serving God for fifteen years, and they're still doing nothing!

Nehemiah was different. He decided to put a deadline to his dreams. He learned to leverage his natural insecure tendencies for the greater good. Although he faced extreme amounts of opposition en route to seizing his God-birthed dream, he never allowed the distractions and discouragement to imprison him.

If you want to fulfill the mission that God has for you, you'd better snuggle up with Nehemiah for the next few weeks. Enter into his world. Imagine things from his perspective. I will do my best to paint the picture with clarity, but you're going to have to take the journey with me. These ten building blocks will challenge you. In fact, they are chiseled out of prayer and pain. But if you take each of these blocks seriously and allow God to mold you, break you, wreck you, and disturb you, you'll see that the progression is natural and altogether exhilarating.

So, if you want to remain a sundial in the shade, that's your call to make. I'm not going to force or beg. However...

- If you want to resurrect God's original dream for your life, continue reading.

- If you want to put your frozen passion on defrost and see God's vision thaw through to your heart once again, get ready.

- If you want to close the gap between your *potential* and *progress* once and for all, then determine to find yourself in the story of Nehemiah and change the world (or at least *your* world) for your generation!

Making It Real:

- Would you consider yourself a sundial
  in the shade? Why or why not?

- What do you want God to do *in* you as you take this journey?
  Write this out in the form of a prayer to your heavenly Father.

DISTURBANCE

BUILDING BLOCK ONE

Building Block 1:

DISTURBANCE

Lord, break my heart for what breaks yours.

A few years ago, my wife Fran and I decided to surprise our two girls, Caroline and Madelyn, with a trip to Disney World in Orlando, Florida. We stayed with my in-laws who live two hours away so we could keep the surprise hidden. We woke up our girls at some ridiculously early hour to buckle their lifeless bodies into their twenty-seven-point safety harness/french-fry storage devices (car-seats).

As you can imagine, our girls, being only five and three, were full of questions:

"Where are we going?"

"What are we doing?"

"Am I dreaming?"

As they came slowly out of their comas, we started telling them, "Girls, we have a surprise for you!"

The dad rulebook failed to warn me for times like this. Screams that raised people from the dead ensued. They were ecstatic for their surprise. They had no idea what we had in store for them.

Fran started asking our oldest daughter, Caroline, what she wanted. Caroline's response was priceless. With sheer glee in her eyes, she said, "Mommy and Daddy, are we going to Wal-Mart to get a new Barbie?" (Now, every dad who's reading this is thinking the same thing. I should have said "Yes!" and saved myself a boatload of money).

"No, we're not going to Wal-Mart to get a new Barbie."

Not phased by that response at all, she said, "Then are we going to Wal-Mart to get me a new booster seat?" Wow. I've got to get my kids out of the house more!

When we realized that we weren't making progress, we pulled over to a rest stop and got out of the car. Fran said, "Girls, the surprise that Daddy and I have planned for you is *not* a new Barbie or a new booster-seat. It is *not* going to Wal-Mart, but instead we… are…going…to…Disney World!" As you can imagine, they totally flipped out. Shrieking hysteria. It was priceless.

The most exotic dream that my girls could muster was to go to Wal-Mart. They couldn't think past a Barbie or a booster seat. Their ideas were so incredibly far away from what we wanted for them at that moment. If we had allowed them, they would have settled. At that time, they wouldn't have known they were settling. But afterwards, if we had told them, they would have been devastated.

I've thought about that car ride conversation many times since. Is this how God sees our lives? Are we satisfied simply dreaming of Wal-Mart? Are we settling for the Barbies and booster seats while the Lord is waiting for us in Disney World? In God's eyes, our dreams are cute and innocent. We're in the backseat, snuggly embraced by our twenty-seven-point safety harness dreaming of walking the toy aisles. These "dreams" are light years removed from Disney World. And that's

The reason so many people never fulfill their dreams: because it was all about them.

the problem. They're *our* dreams. They're wrapped up in *our* world. They are what *we* want. They are what *we* envision. That's why so many people never fulfill those dreams— because it was all about *them*. And, on the rare chance when they do fulfill those dreams, they find the result empty and lacking.

The gravitational pull is towards selfishness.

The problem is that we are self-absorbed. We are thinking about what *we* want and what *our* dreams are. Let's be honest. The gravitational pull is towards selfishness. I'm reminded of the seagulls in *Finding Nemo* shouting "mine, mine, mine" over and over again. As we are going to see, however, God has a different plan. He wants us to live to the fullest by aligning ourselves with what he's doing, not the other way around. Rather than ask him to bless *our* efforts, we should discover what *he's* doing and jump on board. That's what Nehemiah did. And it caught him off guard.

THE CRITICAL ORIGIN OF A DREAM

Every dream that *begins* as a dream will fail. That's right, *fail*. It might be a good idea, but not a God-idea. A God-birthed dream begins not as a dream but as a *disturbance*. The dictionary says disturbance is the "interruption of a settled and peaceful condition." I like to put it this way: *Disturbance is the riot in your soul that aggravates you to move towards something bigger than yourself.* Some call this the "firestorm of frustration" or a "holy discontent." Others call it a righteous indignation. You might call it passion. Regardless, it is this disruption in your heart that sets you onto a new trajectory.

Dreams alone will eventually die of malnutrition due to a lack of spiritual sustenance. If left to itself, it will perish by the virus of discouragement or the frostbite of critics. But a dream that is ignited by, fueled by, and sustained by a Divine Disturbance will not only change the dreamer, it will eventually change the world. It will have the ability to fight off the enemies that commonly attack. It will give you the perspective to make the tough call and to stick it out when your back is against the wall.

I'm not talking about daydreams. Everyone has daydreams. I'm talking about raw, honest, audacious God-birthed disturbances where your heavenly Father has implanted in your soul a divine calling that moves you, stirs you, breaks you and shakes you. Consequently, this disturbance inside of you moves *others* to action as well.

Disturbance is the riot in your soul that aggravates you to move towards something bigger than yourself.

Thus, before long, a movement has begun, and God gets the glory.

You might have felt these promptings from the Lord flow through your soul at one time, but you've allowed negativity and criticisms to sap that river dry. You have buried your divine calling deep under your mattress and are afraid to reach in, dust it off, and discover what you've been missing. Where did it go? How do you know if it's from God?

People obsessed with a Divine Disturbance are different. They're unshakable. Unflappable. Resolute.

Every great man and woman of influence was driven by a Divine Disturbance:

- Martin Luther King Jr. was disturbed about the racial injustice in his world.

- Mother Theresa was disturbed about the pitiful condition of the poor in Calcutta.

- Abraham Lincoln was deeply disturbed
  over the idea of slavery.

I am personally disturbed by the amount of people who never reach their true, God-given potential. It keeps me up at night. I get visibly frustrated when I see someone who has unbelievable potential failing to apply it to a purpose larger than him or herself or next week's paycheck. They are merely a sundial in the shade! Ugh. That's *my* Divine Disturbance.

What's yours?

Maybe you don't know what yours is yet. That's okay.

WHAT IS YOUR THING?

Here's a question that might help:

What is your THING? It's that THING that is inside of you that bugs you. It's that THING that won't let you sleep at night. It's that THING that you know God is leading you to do, start, stop, or lead. It could be a lifelong THING or a short-term THING. Maybe God is prompting you to start a ministry, volunteer on a project, feed the homeless, give money, or write a book. Whatever it is that God has placed on your heart to do is your THING—

It's the DISTURBANCE that God has placed in your heart.

Don't rush this. Don't let the warm fuzzy feeling of a "dream" cause you to leapfrog the first two building blocks. The reason why most people never see these "dreams" fulfilled is because they don't realize that the dream phase is actually the *third* phase of the process, not the first. It's easy to skip. Easy to miss. Tragic to see unfold.

DESTINY

DETERMINATION

DISCOURAGEMENT

DEMONS

DREAMERS

DECLARE

DELAY

DREAM

DEPENDENCE

DISTURBANCE

THE 10 DIVINE DISTURBANCE
BUILDING BLOCKS

That's why we're on this journey together. As we travel side-by-side, I want to walk you through the process of seeing your God-birthed dream become a reality. It is a process. The process is key. The end is not the goal; the process is.

> **The process is key. The end is not the goal; the process is.**

Take heart, you are not alone on the journey.

These are the ten building blocks that we see in the life of Nehemiah as well as in our lives today. As you move from ONE to TEN, you'll discover where you currently are and where you're headed. Let the diagram at the left be a road map for you as you take this journey through the book of Nehemiah.

UNLIKELY HERO

Note: The following is necessary context. Don't get lost.
You'll see why this is important later.

Nehemiah was a man who changed the world for his generation. It all started with a Divine Disturbance in his soul. He became radically disturbed and decided to do something about it. This is his story.

God had a dream for his beloved people, Israel. He had provided a land for them and turned over heaven and earth to see his dream become a reality. But after a great stint of about eighty prosperous years under David's and Solomon's leadership, the kingdom divided under the egotistical rule of Solomon's only son, Rehoboam.

Consequently, ten of the twelve tribes went and settled in the northern region. This was known thereafter as Israel. Two of the twelve tribes settled in the southern region. This was known thereafter as Judah. During this time, the people of God drifted *far* from their heavenly Father. And despite God's full-court press to get their attention by sending prophet after prophet (see the seventeen prophetic books in the Old Testament), neither Israel nor Judah heeded God's call.

God's message through the prophets was simple: either humble yourselves privately before me, or I will humiliate you before everyone publicly!

And he was serious.

Israel (the northern tribes) was destroyed first. In 722 BC, the hideous Assyrians invaded, captured, and disgraced Israel. Actually, *disgraced* is a kind word. Historians tell us that the Assyrians would anally spear their victims, plant the spears vertically in the ground and leave their victim hanging as public signs of submission, torture, and humiliation. Ouch.

Do you think Israel's destruction was a wake-up call to their southern counterpart, Judah? Nope. The Judean tribes continued their worship of false gods, and egotism reached an all-time high. Despite heavy preaching from people like the prophet Jeremiah, they still didn't turn from their sins and pride.

> **God's message through the prophets was simple: either humble yourselves privately before me, or I will humiliate you before everyone publicly!**

So in 605 BC, the great nation of Babylon, led by Nebuchadnezzar, conquered the city of Jerusalem, destroying the buildings, demolishing the temple, burning the city walls, and generally demoralizing everyone there. They captured those who survived the gruesome attack and force-marched them nine hundred miles to Babylon.

Once they had reached Babylon, Nebuchadnezzar and company gave all of Judah's brightest and most gifted leaders full-ride scholarships to BBU—Babylon Brainwash University. There, Judah's elite were taught all things Babylon, given new identities, and heavily encouraged to immerse themselves into Babylonian culture, forgetting their former lives as Jews.

Sadly, most of the people did just that.

But as both Jeremiah and Isaiah had prophesied, at the end of seventy years, the Persians, under the leadership of King Cyrus, conquered Babylon. Cyrus became an instrument in this divine chess game. The Bible says in Ezra 1:1–3 that the Lord stirred the heart of Cyrus to go build the temple of the Lord in Jerusalem. So, being obedient to the stirring in his heart, Cyrus, this pagan king, issued a decree allowing the remaining Israelites living in Babylon to make the nine-hundred-mile (five month) journey back to their homeland so they could rebuild the temple of their God!

Although over two million exiled Israelites lived in Babylon, only fifty thousand took Cyrus' decree to heart and made the journey back.[1] Imagine that. Out of the possible two million, only fifty thousand went back (we'll return to this staggering/sobering fact in a bit).

A few years later, another migration from Babylon to Jerusalem occurred under the leadership of Ezra, the priest. Since the temple was already rebuilt, Ezra's role in the story of God was to help lead the people to worship God in the temple and to restore the priestly function.

Temple rebuilt: check.

Worship rediscovered: check.

Walls reconstructed: not yet.

The people had started worshiping in the temple and praising the Lord again, but the city was still in ruins. No one had taken the initiative to rebuild, especially the city's walls. Ancient cities prized themselves on their ability to protect themselves from outside invasion. So, as you can imagine, the larger the walls around the city, the safer the city stood. Walls around a city meant everything from protection to peace of mind. A lack of strong walls left a city extraordinarily vulnerable to attack. No one wanted to live in a city without walls, even if it was God's holy city–Jerusalem.

No one wanted to live in a city without walls, even if it was God's holy city—Jerusalem.

That's where the story of Nehemiah picks up. Jerusalem was in shambles. The inhabitants were apathetic. No one really seemed to care. No one was disturbed over the condition. No one, except a bartender nine hundred miles away named Nehemiah.

> The words of Nehemiah the son of Hachaliah.
> It came to pass in the month of Chislev, in the twentieth year, as I was in Shushan the citadel, that Hanani one of my brethren came with men from Judah; and I asked them concerning the Jews who had escaped, who had survived the captivity, and concerning Jerusalem. (Nehemiah 1:1–2)

It was an ordinary day for Nehemiah. Drink expensive wine. Eat gourmet food. Rinse. Repeat. As the cupbearer to the King of Persia, his day consisted of testing everything that the king put into his mouth. Poisoning high-level officials was a common practice in 444 BC, making royal cupbearers critical to the longevity of the empire.

As you can imagine, Nehemiah held a pretty important job. He must have been well respected and trusted. Historians tell us that cupbearers often would become close associates with the king—even quasi advisors. How could you spend every meal and snack together with someone for years and *not* get close to them?

Yet one thing was unique about Nehemiah. He was not a Persian. He was a Jew. Obviously his immediate ancestors were not part of the remnant that went back to rebuild the temple, but although he was living in exile nine hundred miles away from Jerusalem, his family's generational hometown, he was very familiar with the city. I'm sure he wondered about it. Dreamt about it. Longed to live there one day.

In the meantime, however, when this story picks up, he was living in the lap of luxury in Susa of all places. Susa was the winter retreat palace for the Persian kings, about two hundred miles north of Babylon. It was breathtaking. It was luxurious. It was vacation.

NEHEMIAH'S DIVINE INTERRUPTION

That's when it happened. That's when Nehemiah's world turned upside down. Unexpectedly. Unplanned. Out of nowhere.

Isn't that how God works in our lives too? When we are the most comfortable, he has a way of pushing us out of the nest. Taking us to the edge of the high dive. Driving us to the brink.

Nehemiah didn't see it coming. Neither will you. News that rocks our world is never predictable. God rarely prepares you for the unthinkable. When tragedy strikes or a death occurs, it's never written in your calendar. Still, God expects you to respond according the measure of faith he has planted inside of you!

> **When we are the most comfortable, God has a way of pushing us out of the nest.**

While in Susa, Nehemiah's brother, Hanani vocalized some awful news:

> "The survivors who are left from the captivity in the province are there in great distress and reproach. The wall of Jerusalem is also broken down, and its gates are burned with fire." (1:3)

Punch in the gut. It had been 150 years since Nebuchadnezzar ransacked the city, and it was *still* a disgrace! In Nehemiah's mind, if God's city was in "reproach" then people were viewing God as a reproach. And this was simply unacceptable. He just couldn't fathom God's city *still* broken down and vulnerable to attack.

Keep in mind, this was before smartphones and the social media. Nehemiah couldn't check his Twitter account to see how the city was doing. He was genuinely clueless about its status. So, when his brother brought to light the brutal facts of reality, it sucker punched him in the midsection.

Images of the city's destruction and rubble flew through his mind. His emotions went crazy.

Hold it in.
Be a man.
Don't lose it.
Ignore it.
Fake busyness.
Help.
No.
Stop.
They need me.
I'm just one man. What can I do?

Ouch. This was not what Nehemiah was hoping to hear on the morning news. I'm sure it took the wind out of him. Maybe he had to sit down. Regroup.

DO YOU REALLY WANT TO KNOW THE BRUTAL FACTS?

Now, when faced with the brutal facts of reality, Nehemiah had a few choices. He could have ignored it and pretended that he never heard it. He could have put it on his "prayer list" and given an empty promise to pray for Jerusalem. He could have shaken his head and said to himself, "those people deserve the lot that they are in—they just need to work harder!"

Similarly, when you and I are faced with the brutal facts of reality, we have the same choices. We can ignore that we ever heard it and continue through life on autopilot. We can *say* that we're putting that tragedy or situation on our "prayer list" but then never enter into the pain of actually praying. Or, we can blame the people for their lack of discipline and work ethic, as if we were superior and have it all together.

Nehemiah was different. When he heard these words, he allowed the brutal facts of reality to rock him, break him, wreck him, and disturb him. He internalized his brother's words. He let them soak in. He weighed the ramifications of the city still being in shambles, and, as one country preacher friend of mine says, Nehemiah was "tore up from the floor up!"

Nehemiah recorded his unfiltered thoughts this way:

> **Nehemiah was different. When he heard these words, he allowed the brutal facts of reality to rock him, break him, wreck him, and disturb him.**

> So it was, when I heard these words, that I sat down and wept, and mourned for many days; I was fasting and praying before the God of heaven. (1:4)

Read those words slowly. Notice:

- "sat down"

- "wept"

- "mourned for many days"

Nehemiah, as we'll see in the coming chapters, was not a weak man. It was not customary for him to weep at the drop of a hat. He was an insanely strong leader, a soon-to-be governor, and a man with a mission. Yet, we see him broken over the news of his city. He was *disturbed* over the condition of his people. Little did he know that these deep feelings were the initial birth pains of a vision that people would be reading about thousands of years later. The point is, Nehemiah's dream didn't begin as a dream. It began as a concern. A burden. A DIVINE DISTURBANCE.

Let's unpack the events of Nehemiah 1:4 one by one.

"When I heard these words…"

He had his ears open for the news. He was actively listening. He was genuinely concerned. When was the last time you actively listened to what someone was saying, instead of having your head buried in your smartphone? Maybe the reason you haven't been *disturbed* about something is because you haven't taken the time to actually *listen* to the world around you. Are you open to actually listening to the needs of the world around you, or are you more concerned about checking boxes off your to-do list? Take some time and listen with an active ear. It could change your life and, consequently, change the world.

"I sat down..."

This news stopped him in his tracks. This was his 9/11 moment where everything changed. His vacation ended. He was no longer the same. In a blink nothing changed but everything changed. He was disturbed. He was broken to the point of inaction. He was divinely paralyzed.

Are you willing to pause your "busy" life and allow the Lord to disturb you?

"and wept..."

An emotional uprising had just surged in his soul. He couldn't "remain professional." When's the last time that you wept over someone else's condition? Can you remember the last time the Holy Spirit rocked you to your core about something or someone? There is something graciously beautiful about snot mixed with a pool of tears in connection to a purpose larger than yourself.

"and mourned for many days..."

This new reality left him shocked and perplexed for days. His mind was spinning. His world was shaken. It was almost as if someone had kidnapped his only child. He was left in awe.

For Nehemiah, his divine dream didn't begin as a dream. It didn't launch as a great idea. He didn't have a marketing plan, a website, and Twitter followers—and merely decided to go a certain direction with his life. No. He allowed the brutal facts of reality to disturb him to the point where DOING NOTHING became his unpardonable sin.

HOW ABOUT YOU?

What are you disturbed about? Is there anything that makes you mad? What makes you frustrated about the world, the church, or your life? I love what Bill Hybels says in his book *Holy Discontent* when talking about this subject. He says, "Still today, what wrecks the heart of someone who loves God is often the *very thing* God wants to use to fire them up to do something that, under normal circumstances, they would never attempt to do."

What can't you stand? What stirs your soul?

Maybe you don't know. That's okay. You need to position yourself on the path where you can be exposed to what God might be up to.

When you become divinely disturbed, something amazing takes place inside of you. You begin to see the world from a completely different perspective. You see through *God's* vision. You might look at the same situation as one thousand others, but *you* see the potential. You see what could be. You see that God has positioned you there to be his point person at this very moment in history.

It doesn't matter if you are flipping burgers or flipping houses. You can be a mechanic or a nurse. What you do doesn't matter. It's what you DO with what you do, that matters. When you are fueled by your frustration, God has you perfectly positioned to receive a dream that *he* wants to birth in you.

> **You might look at the same situation as one thousand others, but *you* see the potential. *You* see what could be.**

SUSA SYNDROME

After reading the previous section, your heart might be stirred to action. You might be tempted to spike your latte in the trashcan like it's the Super Bowl and storm out of Starbucks ready to change the world.

Then reality sets in. Bills are due. The yard needs mowing. Your boss issues her deadline. Your exam is creeping around the corner. Your down comforter is calling your name. You hit the snooze button. Again. Again.

Consequently, you allow those burning feelings of angst to slooowly dig themselves into the familiar graveyard of "shoulda, coulda, woulda's." What happened? Simple. You became comfortable in your captivity.

Remember, Nehemiah—along with about two million Jews who were taken captive 150 years earlier—were technically foreigners. They were *from* Jerusalem but living in exile nine hundred miles away. And when Nebuchadnezzar in 605 BC ransacked the city, he forced the citizens to move to Babylon (modern day Iraq). At first, they were furious. They couldn't believe that "God's people" had been treated this way. However, little by little and year after year, they actually grew to like it in Babylon.

COMFORTABLE IN CAPTIVITY

I'm sure they began to look around and say, "This isn't so bad!" In Jerusalem, they were primarily farmers. Now, they were learning various trades and opening up businesses and becoming accustomed to a new lifestyle. They learned a new language. They adapted to a new culture. They bought houses and erected white picket fences. In a word, they became comfortable.

What they failed to realize was that they were *still* in captivity! They were anything but free. They had bought into the lie and began to believe that they were nothing special. God must have forgotten about them and therefore they were going to live it up while in Vegas.

Take that level of comfort that *most* people were experiencing and put it on steroids. That's the situation in which we find Nehemiah. He's in Susa. It's the winter retreat palace for the Persian kings. Again, his *job* is to test the gourmet food and aged wine. Sign me up! I can't think of a more comfortable gig.

Let's be honest. You and I live pretty comfortable lives. If you are reading this, more than likely you don't have to worry about where your next meal is coming from. You have a roof over your head. You mostly sleep well at night.

Yes, we have stress and some anxiety, but for the most part, our life is pretty comfortable compared to most of the world—especially third-world countries. We live in Susa. Even as I type this, I'm convicted. I'm sitting on my leather recliner, covered with a blanket, next to a warm fire, listening to classical music, and sipping from a huge glass of sweet tea. I'm roughing it!

You might have bought into the lie of the American dream.

The definition of comfortable is "affording or enjoying contentment and security… free from stress or tension." This, my friend, is a trap from the enemy. Let me ask you this, did Jesus die on the cross so that we could be free from stress or tension?

You might have bought into the lie of the American Dream—"buying things you don't need with the money you don't have to impress people you don't like!" That's not a dream. That's a nightmare! And yet, we line up in droves to attain the fleeting desire of comfort.

Is your life's goal simply to be comfortable?

Before you answer that question, look at how you are living your life *now*. Are the decisions you currently make ones that drive comfort or challenge? Are you building your personal Susa?

I've had several conversations with people who are striving to reach a destination of comfort, just to find that they've missed God's best for them. It's like spending your entire life climbing the ladder just to realize, at the end of your life, that your ladder was against the wrong wall!

God doesn't intend us merely to be comfortable, safe, protected, and coasting on autopilot. His dreams for us are far more than escaping pain.

Maybe Susa for you is a *season* of comfort. And sometimes that's okay. We all need a Susa every now and then. But don't let Susa become the norm. Don't dream about Susa. Don't buy into Susa's lies telling you to "eat, drink, and be merry." Don't get to the end of your life just to realize that God had a huge plan for you—a dream for you—but you chose to remain comfortable.

I'm not proud of what I'm about to say, but I must say it to give you context. If I'm honest with myself, for the longest time I allowed the Susa Syndrome to capture my heart. When I heard the news of children dying of malnutrition in third-world countries, I would nod my head with concern, entertain what it must be like to witness that horrendous tragedy daily, say a quick prayer, and then go about my day checking email on my smartphone. When people used to tell me about the sex-slave epidemic in our world *today*, I used to listen with one ear, but with the other ear, I would thank God that those weren't my daughters. When I would watch the evening news and see the homeless of our city, I used to think, "Man, it must be cold this time of year...I hope someone helps them."

Honesty hurts. Even reading back what I just typed is humbling. I was too busy focused on doing ministry for those closest to me that

I neglected what God wanted to do through me for the *world*. I was selfish in my Susa.

That was until I was *rocked* by Nehemiah. This was a guy like me. He was a guy like you (ladies, I'm sure he was like you too). He was going about his day living in luxury until one day he received some news that changed him forever. My prayer is that this book will be your wake-up call. During the two years of writing this manuscript, I've been praying everyday for God to rock you. Shake you. Move you. Disturb you. I've been praying that God will do whatever it takes to get your attention.

> **I've been praying everyday for God to rock you. Shake you. Move you. Disturb you. I've been praying that God will do whatever it takes to get your attention.**

Put this book down if you want to remain the same. Don't read on if you want to remain in Susa. But if you're tired of your spiritual status quo, then tie on your running shoes, and let's go.

I'M SORRY, MR. OSTRICH

Ostriches get a bad rap. You've heard it said that they bury their heads in the sand when the see danger coming. Nope. Urban Myth. Google it.

Do you know who buries their head in the sand of life when confronted with the brutal facts of reality? We do.

Blissful ignorance is *not* a spiritual gift.

Walking around with your head in the sand will not change the world for your generation. You will never fulfill the destiny that God has designed for you unless you begin know the brutal facts of reality. Your dream will always be a solution to a problem in the world. However, you'll never know what problems exist if you don't *ask questions* about it.

Nehemiah chose to ask. His questions were simple. The Bible says it this way:

> I **asked** them concerning the **Jews** who had escaped, who had survived the captivity, and concerning **Jerusalem**. (1:2; my emphasis)

Nehemiah questioned his brother about two things. These two things may look simple on the outset but are pregnant with implications. First, he asked about the people. He wanted to know about the "Jews who had escaped, who had survived the captivity." He was concerned about people. He recognized that people are primary on God's plan.

Question: Who are the *people* in your world that God has placed on your heart? It might be a certain *condition* of people (homeless, spiritually lost, orphans, widows, singles, divorced, etc.) It could be a certain *demographic* of people (elderly, singles, college students, international groups, etc.). Who is God placing on the forefront of your mind?

For me, ever since I became a Christ-follower at the age of sixteen, this one thought has been burned onto my heart: "To inspire leaders to reach their potential, and in doing so, I'll reach mine!" These leaders are *my* people. And, if you're reading these pages, I've been praying for you (*you* are my people too). I've been praying fervently that God will stir a manifesto in your mind and wake you up from your slumber. I've been praying that God will *disturb* you about something, anything. Don't be a sundial in the shade. Reach your potential. Change the world for your generation. Become a champion for Christ!

Not only did Nehemiah ask questions about specific people, but he also questioned his brother concerning the city, Jerusalem. He wanted to know how the city was doing. How was the morale? How were the roads? How was the wall?

Why did Nehemiah want to know about the wall? Remember—without fortified walls, the city was defenseless. Without defenses, God's prized city had remained in ruins for over a century. And that's where his temple stood. That's where sacrifices were made. That's where the presence of Almighty God *used* to reside.

Simply, Nehemiah asked this question: *How can I practically help these people? How can I partner with God's agenda and leverage my God-given gifts and abilities to advance God's mission in my generation?* Little did he know that on the other side of that question was a Divine Disturbance in the waiting. It was a coiled spring ready to launch. It was the first building block for fulfilling a destiny of magnificent proportions.

HOW CAN YOU DISCOVER YOUR DISTURBANCE?

There is something magical that happens when your life begins to live with clarity and focus. When you have extreme focus, the options become fewer and the decisions become easier. Therefore, it is very important that we focus on the following. By focusing on these steps, you'll see them everywhere!

How can you discover your Divine Disturbance?

1. Pray an audacious prayer.

I dare you to pray this prayer everyday for the next thirty days: **"God, break my heart for what breaks yours."** It's that simple. It's that complicated. (I would recommend setting an alarm on your phone for a specific time to do this.) I ask God to break my heart for what breaks his frequently during seasons of focused prayer. It helps tremendously. When you begin to pray this prayer, God will begin to reveal himself and his mission for you in a way that will become crystal clear.

Praying this kind of prayer focuses you. And the object of your focus expands. The more you laser in on seeing God's broken heart, the more you will be overwhelmed with the response.

2. Open your eyes...

Get your head out of the sand. As God starts to reveal to you what breaks his heart, open your eyes to what he might want you to do. Be sensitive to God's Spirit. Remember, God might speak to you in ways other than thunderbolts, lightning, earthquakes, tornadoes, or fires (1 Kings 19). His method usually involves a still, small voice. A whisper. A nudge. A stirring in your soul that you can't shake. Maybe you need to open your eyes to the THING you've been running from all these years. Maybe it's the reason you're not quite whole. You've been a Jonah trying to avoid God's dream for you.

3. Step out...

Get out of your comfort zone. Do something that you would otherwise dodge. Volunteer to help the homeless. Serve. Go on a mission trip. Don't just sit there, do something! It's a lot easier to steer a moving vehicle. You might be tempted to pray about it for long periods of time. I would urge you otherwise. You have no need to pray about getting out of your comfort zone. Get off your blessed assurance and get in the game. The comfort zone is the danger zone.

4. Ask questions...

This might be the most important step. When you ask questions—the right questions, to the right people—the answers might shock you. You might have known about the human trafficking epidemic in our world, but until you started peering into the facts, you had *no* idea it was so bad. You might have realized that homeless people roamed your city. But you didn't know it was *that* bad.

Ask the right questions to the right people—and don't stop until you find the answers that satisfy the divine longing inside of your heart.

MAKING IT REAL:

- As you are praying "Lord, break my heart for what breaks yours" the next thirty days, focus on seeing and sensing the heart of God. Once you see what breaks his heart, seize that moment. Then journal your experiences. Don't hold back. Be honest, open, and raw with your heavenly Father. This could be your hinging moment. Keep it from slipping away. Capture it and let it capture you.

- If you know your Divine Disturbance but have not acted on it, write down five reasons you have remained stagnant. Then write down a prayer that recommits you to the process God originally had for you.

- Talk about this with someone you trust. Vocalize that thing that God has placed on your heart. Even if you can't crystallize all of the details, do the best you can. Now, it's key at this stage that you avoid sharing your dream (you'll see why later). Simply share the disturbance—the thing that has created a riot in your soul and caused a firestorm of frustration.

BUILDING BLOCK TWO

Building Block 2:

DEPENDENCE

"If it is not an impossible thing, it is not a real disturbance."
—*Oswald Chambers*

The essence of Christianity is obedience and dependence. Hear from God. Do what he says. That's obedience. When what he's asking you to do seems impossible, that's where DEPENDENCE comes in. DEPENDENCE is the essence of trust. It is clinging to the person and promises of God.

DEPENDENCE is what Jesus had in mind when he gave his famous "I am the vine and you are the branches" speech to the disciples. This is a tough statement to swallow. Jesus said that "without Me you can do nothing" (John 15:5). Ouch. He didn't say, "Without Me you can do *some* things." He didn't say, "Without Me you can do *good* things." No. Jesus emphatically said, "Without Me you can do *nothing*." Zip. Zilch. Nada. Nothing. Just when you think that you're making ground in your personal or professional endeavors, remember that apart from Christ, you can do nothing!

Nehemiah recognized this reality early and often. He was a man who clung to the Lord. He was desperate. Maybe the problem in your prayer life (or lack thereof) is that you're not desperate enough for the Lord. You have all of your physical, emotional, and social needs met, and you, quite frankly, don't need the Lord. You're not dependent on him because you're not desperate for him. Yet.

The disturbance that welled up inside of this ancient cupbearer started to form it's way into a reality. Nehemiah added opportunity to his anger and it soon jelled in an idea. This idea was so big, so daunting, so incredible that there was no way he could do it—apart from the Lord. He was simply the branch attached to the vine.

I can imagine him looking around the palace and noticing that he, out of all of the people he was close to, was the only one with this unquenchable burden for Jerusalem. He was probably the only one so crazy enough to believe that he, through the strength of the Lord, could actually make a difference.

So he prayed. He prayed dangerous prayers like "use *me* to go rebuild the walls of Jerusalem." He didn't pray for someone else to rebuild. That would be too easy. He prayed for an opportunity to go himself. Prayers like this excite the heart of God.

IS GOD BORED?

Do your prayers make God yawn? Are demons complacent in the presence of your petitions? Are you a prayer worrier or a prayer warrior?

If I had followed you around the past six months and recorded all of your prayers (silent and vocal), what would my journal look like? Would phrases like "be with me" and "keep my family safe" and "bless this food" be listed over and over and over and over? Would my pen be forced to write observations like:

Why are they praying like they don't believe in God?

Where's the power?

Is the God that they read about the same God they pray to?

Tragically, this kind of praying has become the norm. Weak prayers by weak people to a weak God.

I believe that the reason we have grown inept in our prayer lives is because we have grown calloused to DISTURBANCE in our souls. But once we let that disturbance awaken us, we will forever be changed. The gap in the world between what currently *is* and what *could be* cannot be accomplished through human efforts alone. No amount of creativity or ingenuity can accomplish a Divine Disturbance.

> The chasm is too wide.
> The peak is too tall.
> The endeavor is too dangerous.
> The mission is too impossible.
> Apart from prayer.

But Luke 1:37 enters like water splashing us awake from a cozy dream and shouts, "With God, all things are possible."

You're right. You can't do this. That's exactly where God wants you to be. There's a reason why the Hebrew people were backed up against the cul-de-sac of God's providence as their heels were wading in the Red Sea. God had perfectly positioned his people to where the only place they could look was up! And what happened next, we're still talking about today. So it is with your Divine Disturbance. Even though you have yet to articulate it, you know in your soul that this THING is impossible for you to do. If your Divine Disturbance fails to *force* you to your knees in dependent prayer,

The gap in the world between what currently is and what could be cannot be accomplished through human efforts alone.

If your Divine Disturbance fails to force you to your knees in dependent prayer, then it's probably just a good idea, not a God-idea.

then it's probably just a good idea, not a God-idea. It probably came from a planning session, not a providential season.

The disturbance in Nehemiah's soul was nothing short of divine. We see this clearly in what he did with the disturbance. The news *stopped* him in his tracks. Then, due to the magnitude of the situation (the deplorable condition of Jerusalem) he was forced to *drop* to his knees in dependent prayer. It was only after he prayed that he could *roll* his sleeves up and get to work. Stop. Drop. Roll.

That's what God wants to do in your life. He wants to bring you to place where the reality of a situation stops you in your tracks. He wants you to slow down long enough to allow the explosion in your soul to marinate. Then, seeing the magnitude in front of you, he wants you to drop to your knees in dependent prayer. He wants your heart. He wants to hear from *you*. Don't talk to anyone else but the Lord. Lock yourself in a room if you have to. Do whatever it takes. Pray. Commune with the God of the universe. Seek his face. Then, and only then, can you get to the place where you can roll up your sleeves and get to work.

Directly after the news stopped Nehemiah in his tracks, he prayed one of the most honest, God-honoring, earth-shattering, world-changing, prayers recorded in Scripture. Read the following prayer slowly and meditate on what each word means:

> So it was, when I heard these words, that I sat down and wept, and mourned for many days; I was fasting and praying before the God of heaven.
> And I said: "I pray, Lord God of heaven, O great

and awesome God, You who keep Your covenant
and mercy with those who love You and observe
Your commandments, please let Your ear be attentive
and Your eyes open, that You may hear the prayer of
Your servant which I pray before You now, day and
night, for the children of Israel Your servants, and
confess the sins of the children of Israel which we
have sinned against You. Both my father's house and
I have sinned. We have acted very corruptly against
You, and have not kept the commandments, the
statutes, nor the ordinances which You commanded
Your servant Moses. Remember, I pray, the word that
You commanded Your servant Moses, saying, 'If you
are unfaithful, I will scatter you among the nations;
but if you return to Me, and keep My commandments
and do them, though some of you were cast out to
the farthest part of the heavens, yet I will gather
them from there, and bring them to the place which
I have chosen as a dwelling for My name.' Now these
are Your servants and Your people, whom You have
redeemed by Your great power, and by Your strong
hand. O Lord, I pray, please let Your ear be attentive
to the prayer of Your servant, and to the prayer of Your
servants who desire to fear Your name; and let Your
servant prosper this day, I pray, and grant him mercy
in the sight of this man." (Nehemiah 1:4–11)

What jumps out to you from this prayer? What is Nehemiah's attitude towards God? What is his posture? Does a prayer like this resemble your prayers?

THE FIVE AUDACIOUS FILTERS OF DEPENDENCE

Without the mighty favor of God, the wrong you see in the world will never be made right. Without this divine favor, the gap between what currently *is* and what *could be* will never be closed. Nehemiah, when wrecked with the brutal facts of reality, directed his prayers through five audacious filters: Character, Confession, Covenant, Consistency, and Courage. By examining *his* prayer, we find a model for our own.

1. Character – *focus on the character of your heavenly Father*

Nehemiah begins one of the most powerful prayers of Bible this way: "I pray, Lord God of heaven, O great and awesome God..." Wow. Do you really believe that God is great and awesome? You might *say* that you believe that God is awesome, but your actions fail to match what you profess.

One of the major hurdles for living audaciously is knowing who God really is. We misapprehend his character and embrace our own misconceptions instead. Our view is skewed.

One of the books that stopped me in my theological tracks was *The Knowledge of the Holy* by A.W. Tozer. This small book is pregnant with power. Of the many take-aways from this book, one stands out. Tozer quips, "What comes into our minds when we think about God is the most important thing about us." Read that again, slowly.

> **What comes into our minds when we think about God is the most important thing about us.**
> **—A.W. Tozer**

Tozer continues, saying that "We tend, by a secret law of the soul, to move toward our mental image of God." Read *that* again, slowly.

The correlation is thus: Nehemiah's view of the character of God was that he was great and awesome, able to accomplish anything, the God of the impossible, the God who implants and imparts Divine Disturbances to mere mortals and who would help transform this dream into reality.

Is Your View Skewed?

What is *your* view of the character of God? How do you view God, really? Remember, your *view* determines your *actions*. Maybe you've never thought of it this way before, but I believe that your erroneous view of God, as Tozer states, has been the cause of all of your problems.

Here are some common views of the character of God that people have. Where can you relate?

Is Your God a Fun Grandpa?

I saw two bumper stickers on the same car the other day that embodied this view. One said, "Sin now, pray later." The other said, "Lord forgive me for what I'm about to do!" When you view God like a fun grandpa, you act as if he's just going to wink at your actions and give you a check in the mail for your birthday. He'll let you get away with anything because he's trying to be the "cool" grandpa. There are no consequences to your actions. Ever. He's merely a God of unconditional love, without the justice.

Is Your God a Gumball Machine?

I heard someone say recently, "I give money in the offering plate because when I give, I get." His view of God was that God was a gumball machine. Give a little, and he's gonna give a little. Give and take. As long as you do something *for* God, this skewed view says he's obligated to give something in return. He's a fair trade kind of God.

Is Your God a Genie in a Bottle?

God is at your beck and call. He wants to grant your every wish regardless if it aligns with Scripture or not. As long as you pray the right words, with the right inflections, with the right cadence, God is required to make you healthy, wealthy, and whole. You want a God who serves *you*, not the other way around.

Is Your God an Emergency Parachute?

You know that your view of God is the emergency parachute if you find yourself praying prayers like this, "Lord, if you get me out of this one, I promise I'll *never*..." Or, "If you can help me *now*, I promise I'll *always*..." But what happens after God comes through and delivers? Your "never" and "always" get lost in your busyness and you revert back to your way of life before God's merciful intervention. You only need God to help you when your back's against the wall. He's not your leader. He's just your continual deliverer.

Is Your God a Homeboy?

You've seen the t-shirts made famous by Hollywood celebrities. They wear "Jesus Is My Homeboy" memorabilia while getting hammered at parties, engaging in lifestyles completely contrary to the life Christ led. Their actions merely reflect their *perception* of Jesus. If their view of Christ is that he is their homeboy, it makes sense that he would be a club hopping, party going, heavily intoxicated kind of Savior.

Is Your God a Wimp?

Does your God look like Napoleon Dynamite or the Gladiator? Most of us fail to voice courageous prayers like Nehemiah's because we view God as too weak to handle our requests. We have bought into the "Jesus meek and mild" philosophy. Consequently, our actions follow. We control everyone and everything in our lives because obviously God is unable to handle the details. He lacks strength enough to conquer our addictions. He wields insufficient power to restore our marriage. He's inept at resurrecting our finances. So, instead of praying and trusting, we control and stress.

Is Your God an Overstressed Boss?

God is too busy to listen to you. He's got too much on his plate. He's too concerned with pressing world issues to care about your "small" request. (Really? Tell me, what's a *small* request with God? What's a *big* request?) You don't want to bother your busy heavenly Father because obviously he's pacing the streets of gold, worrying about the upcoming election, gun control, terrorism, and nuclear armament. His knuckles must be white with anxiety because his to-do list spirals out of control. He has no time for you. Right. God created time.

Is Your God an Abusive Parent?

Maybe the scars from someone who has done some horrendous things to you have transferred to your heavenly Father. If *that* person abused you (physically, verbally, emotionally) then obviously God *also* treats you like that. You equate the two. And tragically, your actions follow your view. You're afraid. You shrink back. There's a disconnect between the Scriptures and your story. You don't trust. You isolate yourself. You miss out on the abundant life God has for you.

Is Your God a Cosmic Cop?

Have you ever driven with expired license plate tags? I have. When I would see a cop, I would automatically veer off onto a side street, because I just knew that this cop was going to pull me over. Then, from the backseat I would often hear, "Daddy, this isn't the way home! Why did we turn down *that* street?" Ouch.

But sadly, many Christians view their heavenly Father this way. Is this you? Constantly looking in your rearview mirror, you just know that God's going to "get you." Are your actions a direct result of this erroneous view?

Is Your God an Impersonal Force?

According to this view, God is not relational. He's like electricity. He doesn't have a personality. Therefore, why would you pray to an impersonal electrical force? He is not a *he*, rather an *it*. An *it* does not have compassion. An *it* cannot love you. An *it* does not forgive you.

Having read all these skewed views, what is *your* view of God's character? I believe that God is holy, just, all-loving, forgiving, powerful, merciful, gracious, playful, humorous, creative, passionate, sovereign, compassionate, and detailed. My actions therefore are dictated by my view. So are yours.

So, when you pray, remember the character of the one to whom you are praying. For Nehemiah, "great and awesome" were not just words associated with his view of God. They were intrinsically linked to what he *believed* about God. Nehemiah had a supreme view of God. He banked on God's character every time he prayed. And so should we.

2. Covenant – *remind God of his covenant*

As Nehemiah moved down the boulevard of courageous prayer, his on-ramp was God's *Character*. His mile marker one was *Covenant*.

"Lord God of heaven, O great and awesome God, *You who keep Your covenant and mercy with those who love You and observe Your commandments*, please let Your ear be attentive and Your eyes open, that You may hear the prayer of Your servant which I pray before You now..." (1:5–6; italics mine)

By using the name Yahweh (Lord), Nehemiah acknowledged that God never reneges on his promises. It pleases the Lord to hear his children reiterate his promises when they're talking to him.

Remember in chapter one when we talked through the history of Israel? Remember when the city of Jerusalem was attacked by Nebuchadnezzar and exiled to Babylon? Well, there was a prophet named Jeremiah who, *before* the city was attacked, made this prophecy:

"Therefore thus says the Lord of hosts: 'Because you have not heard My words, behold, I will send and take all the families of the north,' says the Lord, 'and Nebuchadnezzar the king of Babylon, My servant, and will bring them against this land, against its inhabitants, and against these nations all around, and will utterly destroy them, and make them an astonishment, a hissing, and perpetual desolations. . . . And these nations shall serve the king of Babylon seventy years." (Jeremiah 25:8–11)

Nehemiah, understanding that God was the one who brought them *out* of captivity, echoed this back to God and reminded God of his covenant with his people. Whereas most people living in the same conditions viewed God's promise as failing, Nehemiah, being divinely disturbed about the situation, viewed exile as God's way of remaining true to his covenant. God promised to do something, and he did it—Nehemiah simply reminded God of his fulfilled promise.

This is what he said:

> "Remember, I pray, the word that You commanded
> Your servant Moses, saying, 'If you are unfaithful, I
> will scatter you among the nations; but if you return
> to Me, and keep My commandments and do them,
> though some of you were cast out to the farthest part
> of the heavens, yet I will gather them from there,
> and bring them to the place which I have chosen as a
> dwelling for My name.'" (Nehemiah 1:8–9)

Yeah, great. But, how do we do pray like this in *our* daily practice? How can we apply these truths, lessons, and principles today?

Here's how reminding God of his covenants might look in your life:

If you need cleansing:

"Father, you have promised in your Word that <u>if I confess my sins</u>, you are faithful and just to forgive my sins and cleanse me from all unrighteousness (1 John 1:9). I claim that now, and I pray that you will forgive, cleanse, and heal me."

If you need wisdom:

"God, your Word says that '<u>if any of you lack wisdom,</u> he should ask of God who gives to all generously without fault and it will be given to him' (James 1:5). I come to you now and seek your wisdom. You've promised to give it to me, and I receive that now."

If you are facing temptation:

"Father, you promised in 1 Corinthians 10:13 that <u>no temptation</u> has seized me except what is common to man and that you are faithful. You will not let me be tempted beyond what I can bear, but when I am tempted, you *will* provide a way out so that I can escape. I need your protection and for you to provide the escape today."

God's Word and his promises are not something to run *from* but to run *towards*. Let this encourage you as you begin to pray audacious prayers for the THING that God has caused to disturb your soul.

We have a tendency to drift.

God needs no reminders in the sense that *he* forgets. He wants to be reminded because he knows *our* tendency to lose alignment with his path and plan. We have a tendency to drift. Praying through the filter of his covenants and promises will undoubtedly resurrect your prayer life.

3. Consistency – *pray day and night, regularly, and systematically*

"(Lord) please let Your ear be attentive and Your eyes open, that You may hear the prayer of Your servant which I pray before you now, day and night." (Nehemiah 1:6)

Vanilla Ice. Milli Vanilli. PSY. What do all of these artists have in common? They are one-hit wonders. For each, all their efforts and accomplishments collided into one memorable song. You have to watch the *Where Are They Now?* television segments to find out about these artist's other music. It's not that they were bad musicians. Well, Milli Vanilli, perhaps. But the others, for whatever reason, were unable to continue to produce at the level of their big hit. This phenomenon got me thinking.

Are you a one-hit wonder in your prayer life? Do you only pray when you *feel* like it? Do you need inspiration prior to your supplication? If so, I want to share with you a quote that I have hanging in my office. It simply says this: "Inspiration is for amateurs!" I'm reminded of this quote every morning at five o'clock when I don't *feel* like getting my big toe out from under the warm comforters and writing a thousand words before work! I use this quote when I don't *feel* like running a few miles each morning. I use this quote when I don't *feel* like praying. I encourage you to do the same.

Because he made prayer a lifestyle, not just an event, he was able to move quickly in the direction he felt the Lord leading him.

Nehemiah had more than a one-hit-wonder prayer life. He was consistent. Systematic. Regular. Methodical. Praying, for Nehemiah, was like breathing. He didn't think about it. It was a natural part of his rhythm. That's why he was able to honestly remind the Lord that he was praying "day and night" (1:6).

In fact he prayed what I call "breath prayers" frequently. These were prayers that he uttered under his breath *as* he was moving *forward*. Because he made prayer a lifestyle, not just an event, he was able to move quickly in the direction he felt the Lord leading him. As you snuggle up next to the story of Nehemiah over the next few days, I want to you to pay special attention to Nehemiah's initial vertical responses (prayer) when life's pressures squeezed him. Prayer was instinctive. It was instantaneous. His immediate reflex was to pray. Praying moved the heart of God, and consequently, changed the world.

Lava Leadership

I am, by nature, consistently inconsistent. I get easily distracted—hey look, a squirrel!—See what I mean?

To combat my tendency to be an octopus on roller-skates, flailing in every direction, always starting and never finishing, I determined to spend an entire year—365 straight days—becoming a person of consistency. I read books on it. I interviewed mentors about it. I listened to every audio book imaginable on the subject. I realized that if I were going to fulfill my Divine Disturbance, it wouldn't happen haphazardly.

A few years ago, during a season of frustration at my *lack* of consistency, I asked one of my mentors, Tim Howey, out to lunch. I said, "Tim, there's a huge gap between my potential and my current reality. I don't want to be one of those guys who has talent, but never gets off the starting blocks because he's not disciplined to see it through. I don't want to be a sundial in the shade. I look at your life and see that you're one of the most disciplined and consistent people I've ever met. You're like a machine! How do I become like that?"

> **He was on fire with passion and methodically moved his influence like lava. Steady. Forward. Consistent.**
> **—Tim Howey**

With a smirk, he put his pizza down and said, "Phil, the leader that you see *today* is not the same leader that was fifteen years ago. I had to grow into a consistent leader. Hey, you need to become more like lava."

I raised my eyebrow in curiosity.

He continued. "I've been listening to a podcast on the ancient Byzantine emperors and their leadership styles—"

I raised *both* eyebrows in curiosity! Where was *this* going?

"They each had various leadership styles," he said. "Some were domineering. Some were political. Some were weak and, therefore, were destroyed. But one of them really intrigued me. His leadership style was described as being like lava. He wasn't flashy. He wasn't sporadic. He was on fire with passion and methodically moved his influence like lava. Steady. Forward. Consistent."

When Tim said that, it struck a chord in my soul. The size of God's dream in my heart for my generation (my Divine Disturbance) was *too* big to remain consistently inconsistent. Therefore, I determined to make consistency in prayer a priority. I told everyone around me for that year that my main goal, my one THING, for that year was to live consistently. The fact that you're reading this book is proof that consistency is powerful. It changed my life and it can change yours.

Old Faithful vs. Steamboat

Think of it this way. What's the most famous geyser in the world? Is it the one that shoots the highest? Longest? With the most force? Nope. It's the one that's the most consistent. Old Faithful in Yellowstone National Park was discovered in 1870 and is famous *not* because of its flash but because of its faithfulness. You can set your watch by its consistency. Every ninety-one minutes it shoots up to 8,400 gallons of boiling water some 150 feet in the air.

Contrast this with the highest shooting geyser in the country, Steamboat Geyser (also in Yellowstone National Park). Although it can shoot twice as high as Old Faithful, it might go up to fifty years without erupting.

Which geyser represents your prayer life? Old Faithful or Steamboat? Consistent or sporadic? Are you waiting on inspiration to get started?

Which geyser represents your prayer life? Old Faithful or Steamboat? Consistent or sporadic? Are you waiting on inspiration to get started? If so, let this be a swift kick in the butt that you need get moving. Get praying! Get consistent!

I've mentioned this before, but if you need assistance remaining consistent, set yourself up for success by placing several alarms on your phone that go off at different times throughout the day. I do this all the time. If I'm in a season when I need to pray for something or someone regularly, I'll put a reminder on my phone at a random time with the caption "pray for Jordan" or "pray or Mom's surgery" or whatever.

Don't be a one-hit wonder. Don't be consistently inconsistent.

4. Confession – *humbly admit your sin*

> "I...confess the sins of the children of Israel which we have sinned against You, and have not kept the commandments, the statutes, nor the ordinances which You commanded Your servant Moses." (1:6–7)

Are you a Heisman Trophy?

For those of you who are college football illiterate, let me explain. The Heisman Trophy is given each year to the best college football player in the country. The trophy itself depicts a running back with one arm sticking straight out, as if to stiff-arm the oncoming defenders. This motion was made famous by Desmond Howard of the Michigan Wolverines who, after a long touchdown run, paused in the end-zone, bent and lifted one knee in the air, held the football against his body with one hand and stuck out his hand in a stiff-arm fashion to pose as if he were the Heisman Trophy.

That pose has become an epic moment in college football. Tragically, though, Heisman

Heisman Christians have become epidemic in the church. We stiff-arm God.

Christians have become epidemic in the church. We stiff-arm those around us—our family, our friends, our spiritual leaders. Sadly, we stiff-arm God. Consequently, we have conditioned ourselves to live plastic lives. Surrounded by images and ads that tell us so, we have trained our minds to believe we can't be real. We don't have the capacity to be honest.

So what do we do? We fake it. "We fake it till we make it!" We fake it with those we love. We pretend that we have everything together. We put on the show for everyone and give the appearance that we don't need help. That we're okay. That everything is great.

We are lying.

We are lying to ourselves. We are lying to others. We are lying to God.

Not only are we lying, but we are *miserable.* When David sinned with Bathsheba and was running from God, do you think he was happy? No. In fact this is what he said about that time period when he posed as a Heisman trophy.

> When I refused to confess my sin, my body wasted away, and I groaned all day long. Day and night your hand of discipline was heavy on me. My strength evaporated like water in the summer heat. (Psalm 32:3–4; NLT)

Is *your* body wasting away? Are you groaning inwardly all day long? Has your strength evaporated like water in the summer heat? If so, you might be experiencing the consequences of withholding confession from your heavenly Father. He wants you to come clean. He wants you to live a life that's free. It's impossible to live a life wholly surrendered to your Divine Disturbance when you are clutching unconfessed sin and its consequences and stiff-arming the one who can free you from it.

I'm sure that during the 150 years after Jerusalem's walls were destroyed, other men and women had dreams of restoring God's city. But, as we will see, Nehemiah was different. Rather than blame others, he confessed. He wasn't a Heisman Leader. He was a man who humbly confessed *his* sin as well as his nation's sin. He refused to point fingers. His heart was broken for his role in the mess.

Yes, confession is messy. That's why it's so hard for us to do. We like to live our pretend lives and hide. We are insecure. Our insecurity forces us to hide behind our stuff and our looks and our kids' accomplishments and anything else that will keep God and others at an arm's length. We want to be defined by what we *do* instead of who we *are* because what we are is insecure.

Yes, confession is messy.

We adopt a plastic exterior because we don't think that God will accept us "as is." We are trying to prove to the one who knows everything that we have it all together. We don't need his help. We can do this all on our own. We might be afraid that if we let God into that chamber in our hearts, he might disown us. Abandon us. Chastise us. Stop loving us. We treat God like we do everyone else. And so, we keep on pretending and giving God the Heisman stiff-arm. Keeping him at an arm's length.

What happens when you and I do that? We settle for the shadow instead of the substance. Our lives are marked by plastic instead of purpose. The Divine Disturbance that God has placed in our hearts will remain only a fantasy and never come into fulfillment.

Confession is a beautiful thing. It cleanses. It frees. It heals. Conversely, the lack of confession binds. It hijacks. It suffocates.

Confession is a beautiful thing. It cleanses. It frees. It heals.

Contrary to some of your misconceptions about confession and repentance, our heavenly Father desires us to confess to him and to others—not out of obligation or interrogation tactics—but because of what it does for his relationship with us and our relationship with others.

As an NFL Chaplain, I try to make every chapel service memorable for the players and coaches. The spiritual spectrum among the men is pretty wide. Some guys are sold-out, all-in. They love Jesus and everyone knows it. Others simply attend our chapel services because they think it's a good luck charm. Therefore, one of my goals in communicating God's truth to these guys is to make what I say stick. Make it memorable. I almost always lead chapel service with some kind of visual aid.

So when I preached on the power of confession, I filled a three-foot glass container with water and placed it on a table in the middle of the room. Then I passed out little business-card sized pieces of rice paper to all the guys. At the end of my message, I had them all take about three minutes to write on the paper something that they needed to confess to the Lord. When they finished, they folded their papers and put them in a box. I took the box and slowly poured the papers into the water. As I poured in the folded slips, I took a wooden spoon that had been soaking in red food coloring and stirred. It turned the whole glass container red. As I moved the wooden spoon around and around, the pieces of rice paper started to disintegrate, and, eventually, they all disappeared. It was a movement that I'll never forget. Men the size of refrigerators, idolized by the public, were brought to snotty tears over the power of confession.

What would you write down on that piece of transparent rice paper?

Don't Blame Others

If you read Nehemiah's confession carefully, you see that he includes himself in the national confession. Even though he is far removed from the transgressions of the past and the ineptitude of the people currently living in Jerusalem, he uses the word "we." He says, "I ... confess the sins of the children of Israel which *we* have sinned against You..." (1:6). He didn't shrink back from confessing his sin. We must do the same.

While I was on a writing trip trying to finish up this manuscript, my wife kept sending me video links to watch the various speakers and worship from an amazing women's conference in Austin, Texas, that she had attended called the "IF: Gathering." One of the speakers, Christine Caine, struck a chord in my soul. She was talking about how the Hebrew people in Exodus were content to be delivered from bondage out of slavery but too content to live in true freedom. So they turned an eleven-day journey into forty years of wandering in the wilderness. They accepted deliverance from Egypt, but didn't embrace freedom by entering the Promised Land. Whew.

In our lives, when we don't keep a short confession account with the Lord, we, too, accept deliverance without embracing freedom. Yes, we are set free and heaven bound, but our lives are still marked by the chains of unconfessed sin.

A Time to Confess

Take some time now and confess to your heavenly Father. Don't stiff-arm him anymore. He wants you to be real. Honest. True. It's okay if this is painful. There is progress in the pain.

Do you need to confess:

Sin

Motives

Actions

Thoughts

Lying

Family history

Personal history

Do you need to confess to someone else?

I want to encourage you to do business with God. Stop reading. Pause. Reflect. What you do over the next few minutes will set the trajectory of the rest of your life. Don't hurry this process. Wait. Be still. Cry if you need to. Journal. Embrace this moment.

5. Courage – *audacious, God-honoring, knee-trembling requests*

> "Let Your servant prosper this day, I pray, and grant him mercy in the sight of this man." (1:11)

Finally, the section on *courageous* prayers! Nehemiah was audacious enough in his requests to actually believe that God was who he said he was and that he would do what he said he would do. It is only after we realize the first four steps in the praying process that we can come to this moment of courage.

This step is where our generation gets the process backwards. We are the entitled generation, and so we start with courageous requests and bold proclamations to our heavenly Father. Yet we ourselves are void of substance. If God were to grant us the requests we utter so flippantly, we would not be able to handle the weight of such responsibility. That's why the first four steps in Nehemiah's prayer journey are so critical. They are essential to building the person behind the dream, not just the dream itself. If the dream is realized apart from the dreamer being more Christ-like, then the dream will be null and void.

Having that backdrop in mind, think of the audacity of Nehemiah's attitude towards God. He said, in essence, "God, I believe that you have perfectly positioned me to be your change agent in my generation. You have set me up with the perfect relationship with the King. He trusts me implicitly. I have proven faithful. Now, I ask that you leverage this relationship for *your* glory. Let *me* be the one who rebuilds Jerusalem's walls. Let *me* be the one who leads your people back to spiritual and physical prosperity. Let *me* be your man for the job. I recognize that I'm not qualified. I'm not an official. I'm not a ruler. I'm definitely not a construction worker. I'm not a 'leader' in people's minds. I'm simply a cupbearer. Yet you have never called the equipped. You equip the called. I believe that you have called me for this role. My calling is birthed out of a Divine Disturbance in my soul that I cannot shake. It keeps me up at night. It consumes me. And it is out of the overflow of this Divine Disturbance that I boldly

> **We are the entitled generation, and so we start with courageous requests and bold proclamations to our heavenly Father.**

pray for your divine favor for this task. Let your gracious hand be with me and grant me success."

Courageous prayer by a courageous man.

Again, this goes back to our view of God. If our view is skewed, our prayers will limp along. I love what Mark Batterson says in his book, *The Circle Maker.* He says,

> Bold prayers honor God, and God honors bold prayers. He is offended by anything less. If your prayers aren't impossible to you, they are insulting to God. Why? Because they don't require divine intervention. But ask God to part the Red Sea or make the sun stand still or float an iron axhead, and God is moved to omnipotent action.[2]

I'm sure that when you read that last quote, your heart started beating a little faster, as did mine. We get excited about the future and believe, for a moment, that God is big enough to do the impossible. What if you were able to live *continuously* with that feeling of optimism in the person and power of God? You can.

Recently, I preached a Christmas message called "Are You a Christmas Atheist?" The sermon built on the idea that we sing the cute Christmas songs and enjoy the festivities around the holiday, but our lives don't measure up to the words coming out of our mouths or the decorations around our homes. My text was Isaiah 9:6, which says, "And His name will be called **Wonderful, Counselor, Mighty God, Everlasting Father, Prince of Peace.**" Here's what I said:

My calling is birthed out of a Divine Disturbance in my soul that I cannot shake.

You Might be a Christmas Atheist if...

- You believe Jesus is **Wonderful**, but just not in *your* life.

- You believe Jesus is the great **Counselor**, but you rarely pray or seek his Word for counsel.

- You believe Jesus is the **Mighty God**, but doubt his power on your behalf and try to control everything and everyone.

- You believe Jesus is the **Everlasting Father**, but to you he's more of a figure, not a Father.

- You believe Jesus is the **Prince of Peace** in theory, but your life is marked by worry, stress, and fear.

If you recognized yourself in these statements, let me echo for you the super-spiritual, highly educational ESPN TV show that airs in the fall called *Monday Night Countdown*. Each week they have a segment called "C'mon Man!" where they broadcast the top bonehead plays of the previous week. After showing the clip, all of the commentators shout in unison, "C'mon Man!" Here are some "C'mon Man!" scenarios for you:

- You may believe that this mighty God could part the Red Sea and deliver two million Hebrews out of slavery, but you don't believe him to part the Red Sea of your life to deliver you (or your loved ones) from the slavery of addiction! **C'mon Man!**

- You may believe that this mighty God could raise Lazarus back from the dead but you don't believe that he can raise your finances, or marriage, or career out of the grave. **C'mon Man!**

- When you hear sermons about Jesus calming the storms and walking on water, you shout, "Amen, Amen," but when the storm rages and lightning strikes in your life you worry, you stress and say "He can't, he can't!" **C'mon Man!**

- You believe God's mighty power saved Shadrach, Meshach, and Abednego from the fiery furnace, but you laugh at God's ability to rescue you from the cauldron of depression, loneliness, suffering, or diseases of heartache and pain. **C'mon Man!**

- You believe the song "He's Got the Whole World in His Hands," but you control every corner of your world and password protect your mighty plans against access by the Creator. **C'mon Man!**

- You sing the lyrics "Savior, He can move the mountains, My God is mighty to save,"[3] but when a mountain looms before you (whether it's a relational mountain, family mountain, financial mountain, or medical mountain) you worry and stress and don't really believe what you sing about. **C'mon Man!**

It's time to trade in your erroneous view of God for the God of the Bible. He is the God of the impossible. That's what he does. That's who he is. DEPENDENT prayer is essential to seeing and seizing the Divine Disturbance that God has placed in your soul. You can't achieve it without God's intervention. Your heavenly Father wants you to *consistently* pray through his *character*, reminding him of his *covenant*, keeping an honest *confession* while *courageously* approaching his throne of grace! This is prayer. This is where the real work happens.

MAKING IT REAL:

- Nehemiah prayed through five filters. Which one stands out to you as an area needing improvement in your prayer life?

  Character, Covenant, Consistency, Confession, Courage

- To which of the views of God (grandfather, parachute, etc.) do you relate the most? Why? Or list another unmentioned example of a skewed God perspective. How does this view of God impact how you live and pray?

- If we were to write a "C'mon Man!" skit for your prayer life, what would we be forced to write?

- Take some time now and pray authentically. Use this time to recommit yourself to praying through your Divine Disturbance.

BUILDING BLOCK THREE

Building Block 3:

DREAM

This is our permission to dream big dreams.
For small dreams neither stir the hearts of men nor of God.

The pregnancy phase is complete. After DISTURBANCE and DEPENDENCE incubate, then—and *only* then—your God-birthed DREAM is ready to come into this world. This DREAM becomes your true north—your magnificent obsession. This is your magnum opus—your lifelong work. Sadly, many of us have forgotten how to dream. Yes, we dream at night, but the most powerful dreams occur when we are wide-awake.

Remember when you were a child? Innocent. Pure. Adventurous. Able to dream the most ridiculous dreams imaginable. Nothing was impossible for you. *Can't* was never in your vocabulary. You were creative. You were passionate. You were brilliant. You were six.

But then something started to happen. Teachers started telling you to color within the lines. Parents started hedging you inside fences. Peers started laughing at you if you were just a bit different. And worst of all, you started listening to the little voice in your head telling you that you needed to fit in, conform, blend, be average. That you shouldn't express any dream welling up inside of you because the

Many of us have forgotten how to dream. Yes, we dream at night, but our most powerful dreams occur when we are wide-awake.

moment that you did, it would get crushed by others.

So, you buried your dreams under the rug of safety. For when your dreams were hidden, no one could ridicule them. Criticize them. Pick them apart and recite a list of reasons why they were ludicrous. You believed the doubt. Doubt led to inaction, and you successfully paralyzed yourself. Yes, all of your physical limbs might have been functional, but your dream muscles withered and your vision lenses fogged.

Is this assessment resonating with you? I hope so.

It is *way* easier to play it safe. It is easier to live comfortably in Susa. But somewhere in the distance God is calling you for a greater life. He wants you to resurrect that dream that *he* placed inside of you. He wants you to come alive. I've heard it said that the glory of God is man fully alive. Are you *fully* alive? Or are you simply breathing? There is a world of difference between those two realities.

Fully Alive	Simply Breathing
Purposeful living	Surviving through life
Activated by a dream	Coasting—hoping to blend in
Passionate	Passive
Contagious	Cantankerous

If I were sitting across the table from you, I would look you in the eye and tell you that today **I give you permission to dream big dreams. For small dreams neither stir the hearts of men nor of God.** I give you the permission I once desperately needed and received from an unexpected source. Let me explain.

I QUIT!

A few years ago, 2010 to be exact, I wanted to give it all up. Throw in the towel. Get out of the ministry. My part-time job was senior pastoring a large church. My full-time job was feeding three large meals each day to the demons of doubt that had taken up residence in my mind. Not only did these demons of doubt need meals, but they needed comfort, attention, and time—all of which I gave liberally. I made sure they were tucked in at night and woken early in the morning. I was a great host.

Or so I was until I met some new friends who were able to snap me out of the funk I was in. (More on this in Building Block 8 – Discouragement. It's a *must read* chapter.) Benson and Kristen Sexton had gone through more in their two years of marriage than most people do in a lifetime. One year after they were married, Kristin became pregnant with their baby boy, Luke. But during the sonograms, the doctors discovered that baby Luke had a rare heart defect called hypoplastic left heart syndrome. Basically, he had a half-functioning heart. When Luke was born, the doctors quickly realized that his defect was worse than they had originally thought. Luke lived a strong twelve days and then, while in the arms of his loving mother, he met Jesus. The Sextons blogged about their experience during their deepest pain, and soon the world became surrogate parents of baby Luke. People from around the world started commenting how Luke's twelve-day life had given them perspective—and hope—that God loved them and had a plan for their lives. Wow. Humbling. Breath-taking.

The first time I met Benson and Kristen was at baby Luke's funeral. I went, not as a pastor, but as someone touched by their story and in awe of their resilience. The casket lay up front, hardly bigger than one of my shoe boxes. I found my seat on the back pew and sat in wonderment as people shared story after story about the impact that this little boy had made on them.

Then it happened. The pastor stepped down, and Benson, Luke's father, stepped up to the microphone to lead everyone in Chris Tomlin's worship song "I Will Rise." I didn't know what to do. I usually pride myself for being able to handle myself in any situation. Not this time. Do I sing? Do I watch? Do I stare at the hymnal and Bible that are in the pew in front of me?

You believed the doubt. Doubt led to inaction, and you successfully paralyzed yourself.

As Benson began to sing Tomlin's words about a "peace" he'd "come to know" and the soul-anchor that allowed him to say "it is well" despite his grief, I looked through my tears and saw Kristin, this twenty-three-year-old mother, who had just lost her baby boy, *standing* on the front row with both arms reached towards heaven, *worshipping* her heavenly Father! Soon, no one sat. Everyone, with arms stretched heavenward, worshipped God in tearful harmony.

This was one of the most powerful moments of my life. I *had* to meet these people. They must have known Jesus in a way that I had only read about. When we finally did meet, my assumptions were confirmed. Not only were they passionately in love with Jesus, they were as desperate for friendship as my wife and I were. Thankfully, we not only met but became best friends. Keep in mind, I was at an extremely low point in my life and leadership.

During our first "double date" to the local Mexican restaurant, I started telling the Sextons my feelings of doubt and insecurity as a leader. I shared with them that maybe I wasn't cut out for pastoring. Maybe I missed my calling. Maybe this whole ministry idea was a good idea but not a God-idea.

After courteously listening to my ramblings for a few minutes, Kristin grew visibly upset. Oh great, I thought, I just said something offensive in her moment of deepest sadness. I'm such jerk.

She looked at me—no she looked *through* me—and with her one-of-a-kind southern accent while pounding on the table, she said, "Phillip Kelley, you be quiet now and listen to me. I've listened to you go on and on about how you might not be *called* into this ministry and that you're not cut out for this. I've been patient with you as you talked through your doubts and insecurities. But now it's my turn."

> **The same God who comforted me while I held my baby boy as he met Jesus will comfort you through this time and pull you out of this!**
> **—Kristen Sexton**

I stopped chewing. Oh boy. I had just angered the wrong southerner.

"Let me tell you something, *pastor*." (She used that title mockingly). "This might be the first time that the four of us have met together, but I think that it's for *this* reason. God wants me to tell you that you need to walk in your authority that *he* has given you. Don't you dare doubt your calling, your ability, or the hand of God on your life. Dream big. Pray for audacious visions. The same God who comforted me while I held my baby boy as he met Jesus *will* comfort you through this time and pull you out of this! Now, it's time to snap out of it. Quit whining. Quit feeling sorry for yourself. You're better than this!"

I felt like I was in a time-out, holding my blankie in the corner. What had just happened? How should I respond? I was being scolded by a twenty-three-year-old, little blonde girl I had just met. Well, that day became a turning point in my perspective. In fact, at the end of our dinner, I grabbed one of the napkins and wrote this contract:

**"This is our permission to dream big dreams.
For small dreams neither stir the hearts of men nor God!"**

I dated it, and we all signed the napkin. I framed my copy. Here it is:

Interestingly, when we moved away from that city, Kristin made the following picture for us and wanted it to be the first picture I hung in my new office. It means more to me than most anything. It is a daily reminder to dream big dreams. Live by faith. Press on.

So let me ask you. Are you running from the dream that God has placed on your heart? Is *doubt* your daydream? Is *second-guessing* your Snuggie? Is *fear* your friend? If so, maybe it's time we go for some Mexican food, and I will tell you what Kristin told me.

God has made you for great things. There is no one like you on the planet. No one has your unique story. He has set you up for great things (even if that greatness is merely being faithful in the small things—often the faithful ones are the greatest champions of them all). If you're doubting, stop it. If you're afraid of rejection, leverage that fear for passion in your work. Stop using your incredible brain to think up elaborate rationalizations and justifications for avoiding

The only difference between the rut and the grave is its depth.

action! Start. Start somewhere. But start. Get moving. The only difference between the rut and the grave is its depth. Snap out of it. Let God comfort you *while* you are working toward his dream.

LEVERAGING THE TENSION

This is the tension that Nehemiah faced. He was disturbed over the pitiful condition of Jerusalem. He begged God in dependent prayer to forgive the people and remember his covenant with them. Now, Nehemiah started to receive God's dream with clarity. He became consumed with being the one to go and rebuild Jerusalem's walls. It would be an audacious undertaking. But he was struck with the tension of what currently *was* and what *could be*. That's how a DREAM is birthed. When you embrace the disconnect between the current reality of a situation and the potential of it, a God-birthed dream begins to form.

- You might see the disconnect between where your marriage is and where it could be…

- You might see the divide between where your finances are and where they could be…

- You might see a gap between the life orphans could have and the life that they currently have…

Andy Stanley, in his amazing book *Visioneering*, says this:

> Anyone who is emotionally involved—frustrated, bro-kenhearted, maybe even angry—about the way things are in light of the way they believe things could be, is

a candidate for a vision. Visions form in the hearts of those who are dissatisfied with the status quo. Vision often begins with the inability to accept things the way they are. Over time that dissatisfaction matures into a clear picture of what could be.[4]

The idea of rebuilding the wall of Jerusalem consumed Nehemiah. It was his elevator speech. It was his midnight prayer. It was what he doodled while killing time. He recognized that it was crazy. But that didn't stop him. When King Artaxerxes asked him "What do you request?" Nehemiah's immediate response was, "I ask that you send me to Judah, to the city of my fathers' tombs, *that I may rebuild it*" (Neh. 2:4–5). He was clear. Concise. Confident. He knew exactly what God wanted him to do. And when the moment of truth came, he boldly stated his DREAM (more on this later).

GOOD IDEA OR GOD-IDEA?

Okay, now you realize that a God-birthed dream is something that moves you, stirs you, rocks you, and disturbs you to the point of action. That's great! But how can you know if it's a good idea or a God-idea? Now is a good time to double check that you've avoided leaning that ladder against the wrong wall.

Not only do we need a DREAM, but we need clarity that this dream is the one for us. As Marcus Buckingham says, "Clarity is the antidote to anxiety."[5] If you want to be anxiety free, be clear about the dream that God has for you and align everything that you do with that true north. When your DREAM is clear, the options become fewer and the decisions easier.

> **Clarity is the antidote to anxiety.**
> **—Marcus Buckingham**

FASTING BRINGS CLARITY

This kind of clarity only comes through climbing the first two building blocks of DISTURBANCE and DEPENDENCE. In the last chapter I purposefully neglected to mention one little phrase from Nehemiah 1:4. Let's see if you can catch it:

> So it was, when I heard these words, that I sat down and wept, and mourned for many days; *I was fasting* and praying before the God of heaven. (Emphasis mine.)

Okay, I made it easy for you. Nehemiah didn't just pray. He *fasted* and prayed. He deprived his body of something physical to focus on the spiritual. He was desperate for God to move, and he needed divine clarity. Fasting brings clarity. It removes the junk out of our lives and gives us a hunger for God like never before. Some people might object and say, "Seriously, you've taken this far enough. You want me to give up *food* for this?"

Fasting removes the junk out of our lives and gives us a hunger for God like never before.

Really? List one thing that's more important than fulfilling your God-given destiny. Go on. I'm waiting.

One of my mentors is Dr. Elmer Towns, co-founder of Liberty University. He has been a giant in the faith to me, modeling prayer and fasting for eight decades! In his book, *Fasting Can Change Your Life*, Towns writes, "The Hebrew word for fast comes from *tsome*, which implies distress—we are so distressed that we lose our appetites. Some fast to touch God; others fast after they have seen God."[6]

My prayer is that you do both in the days to come. I pray that you will fast to touch God. You want *to see* him more clearly. You want to enter into his majestic presence and bathe in his glory! I'm also praying for some of you to fast because *you have seen* God move mightily among you. I'm praying that you are so disturbed over what disturbs the heart of God, so ruined by his renown that you can't help but fast. This type of fast is in response to, not in request of.

Fasting gets ourselves in alignment with what God wants to do in us, through us, and for us. It's not about getting God to do something or causing him to change his mind. It is merely aligning with him (to partner with him) to do what he has purposed from the beginning to do. When we fast, we don't get more of God. When we fast, God gets more of us.

ALIGNMENT ISSUES

As of this writing, my car constantly veers to the right. If I don't course correct, I will end up in the ditch every time. I need to take my vehicle and get the wheels aligned. That's what fasting does. It brings us back into alignment with God. It brings our lives and the dream that God has for us into focus.

Let's keep with the driving analogy. If you take a ride with me in my car, I guarantee that I'll have stacks of motivational or leadership CDs in the passenger seat that I'm listening to at the moment. I'm obsessed with learning and growing as a leader, communicator, and pastor. But occasionally, I'll turn on the radio to work on my driving dance moves. "The sprinkler" is a classic stoplight routine for yours truly.

When your articulation of your dream is fuzzy and full of static, you're in for a miserable journey.

And while getting my grove on at a red light, I get frustrated to hear static. Static, while doing the Carlton and embarrassing everyone riding with me, is unacceptable. Fuzziness from the airwaves makes the drive miserable for everyone involved. Likewise, when your articulation of your dream is fuzzy and full of static, you're in for a miserable journey.

Fasting moves us. It brings us into agreement *with* God, alignment *to* God, and sets up our assignment *for* God.

Have you ever fasted for divine clarity? Nehemiah did. I want to challenge you to do likewise. You can choose from a variety of fasts. You can fast like Daniel, eating just fruit, veggies, and water for twenty-one days. I try to do this in January every year. It's a powerful way to start the year. Obviously you can fast from food (but if you go more than a few days, always consult your doctor first). Media fasts also help unclutter your life and get you back in alignment with God's vision. What if I took your precious Facebook addiction away from you for a few seconds, hours, days, weeks? Don't you think that you'd be able to listen better to the voice of God if it weren't crowded out by how many "likes" you received or "retweets" you got on some pithy statement you shared?

The primary goal of your fast should be to know God more. When you deprive yourself of something physical to focus on something spiritual, the static is removed from God's broadcast. It's a powerful exercise.

DEVELOPING GOD'S D.R.E.A.M.

DISTURBANCE and DEPENDENCE transition naturally into the discovery of your DREAM. But they go hand in hand. You can't have a DREAM without the first two building blocks supporting it. The rest of this chapter functions more like a workbook than a chapter. I want you to take this seriously. The questions that I'm having you ask yourself are meant to force you to focus on the DREAM that God has for you. You might need to get away and have a personal retreat so you can have what I call a DAWG. (Day Alone with God). We'll use the acronym *D.R.E.A.M* as our outline to clarify your God-birthed dream.

D: Desire – *The "what" of your DREAM.*

The Bible says in Psalm 37:4 to "Delight yourself also in the Lord, and He shall give you the desires of your heart." If we are walking in the ways of God, being filled with his Spirit and striving to obey his every promptings, we can rest assured that our desires are going to align with God's desires. The burden that he has placed on your heart to accomplish did not originate within your own mind.

The "what" of God's dream for you is going to be larger than you've ever imagined. We serve a big God with limitless possibilities. Remember, if the size of your dream is not intimidating to you, it's probably insulting to God. I'm sure that Nehemiah sat there wresting with his own inadequacies as a leader when God placed within him the desire to go rebuild the wall of Jerusalem. He wasn't a builder. He was bartender. He wasn't a construction worker. He was a cupbearer. But the desire rose from within. He couldn't shake it. He couldn't stop thinking about it. It became his magnificent obsession.

What would you attempt if you knew you would not fail?

Let me ask the question this way. What would you attempt if you knew you would not fail? Maybe you haven't let your mind go wild with imagination like this lately because you've buried your dream under the rug of safety and comfort for too long. Pull up the rug. Bring out your dream. Dust it off.

What's the desire inside of you? Take some time to reflect on that. Write it out. Go ahead. I dare you to dream big DREAMS! For small dreams neither stir the hearts of men nor of God.

R: Reason – *The "why" of your DREAM.*

When you know your "why," you'll discover your way. What is the reason behind your desire? If it is purely selfish, you'll know that this might be a good idea, but not a God-idea. Ask yourself *why* you want to accomplish this or that. What's the larger purpose? Often we focus on building our own "Thingdom"—the creature comforts of our first-world society. But God wants us to be about his Kingdom. Is your desire for God's Kingdom or merely your own Thingdom?

Is your desire for God's Kingdom or merely your own Thingdom?

When you answer the "why" behind the "what," it adds motivation to your determination. Trust me, you'll need to revisit your "why" often, because, as we'll see throughout the story of Nehemiah, it's going to get difficult to press on. In the midst of difficulties, confusion, disappointments, and discouragement, reminding yourself of the reason "why" you even got yourself into this mess might be your only saving grace.

So go ahead. Take some time to write down *why* you want to pursue your God-birthed dream. (It will probably stem from your original DISTURBANCE.)

E: Experiences – *The "who" of your DREAM.*

I almost nixed writing this book because I figured that the world already had good books on the subject of Nehemiah and didn't need to have *another* one. Yet, after a season of prayer, fasting, and listening to advice, I became convinced that even though I thought I might be redundant, no one on the planet had my same experiences. I am unique. As Psalm 139:14 says, "I am fearfully and wonderfully made."

You might feel the same angst about your DREAM. You might feel that you are nothing special. You have a plain-Jane life. But God has uniquely wired the *you* of you. Your experiences—your past, present, and future—perfectly align you to fulfill your unique calling. You'll do it better than *anyone* else, because they're not *you*.

From Cleaning Tanning Beds to Tackling Terrorists: JJ's Story

Let's take JJ's story for an example. JJ is one of my best friends. He works for the FBI in undercover intelligence. He has a separate work identity complete with social security number, address, license, and credit "history." He's one of those guys who can never tell anyone where he works, what he does, or who he's with. Well, I guess he *could* tell you. But then he'd have to kill you. JJ specializes in counter-terrorism and surveillance operations. He's on the front lines and leads a team to tackle some pretty crazy stuff. I catch myself trying to live vicariously through him.

We were talking the other day about this chapter, and he told me the story of how he got his job in the FBI. He said one of his first jobs out of college was a tanning salon manager. (As I typed that last sentence, I chuckled so loudly the guy sitting next to me on the airplane looked over to see if I was okay). If you knew JJ, you'd pick him as the last guy on the planet to manage a tanning salon. JJ said, "Phil, every day at work was the worst day of my life." For two agonizing years he had to manage dozens of high-school-aged workers

> Phil, every day at work was the worst day of my life.
> —J.J.

and their chaotic shifts, in an environment that was anything *but* glamorous.

His dream was to serve our country in the FBI and defeat bad guys. You can see why cleaning tanning beds and selling lotion was the bane of his existence. When the opportunity opened to interview for the FBI, he jumped on it. It was his desire. He was DISTURBED after 9/11 and this passion fueled his *"why."* But he was worried about his lack of experience.

That's why he was shocked when he got the call from the supervisor saying that the hiring choice came down to him or another guy. The FBI decided to choose JJ. Why? He had *management experience* and the other guy didn't! Who would have thought that the one circumstance he thought would prevent him from doing his dream job was actually the catalyst for receiving it!

That's how God uses our experiences to leverage his purposes. Let me ask you this: What experiences has God placed in your path that might be beneficial to fulfilling your God-birthed dream? Good experiences and bad. You might have tried to forget them. But those experiences have shaped you into who you are today. Don't neglect them. Embrace them. For in these experiences, God might be shaping your future.

Nehemiah's experience as a cupbearer placed him inside the circle of influence necessary to pull off his DREAM. He had a network list that put LinkedIn to shame. Why? Because God set up the script perfectly. No doubt Nehemiah had enormous amounts of leadership capabilities. I'm sure he questioned *why* he was serving food and wine before the king when he wanted to be out doing something GREAT. Little did he know that God would soon leverage his experiences for something truly magnificent.

A: Abilities – *The "how" of your DREAM.*

God designed everyone with a set of abilities. These are the skills that come naturally to you. Do you have a natural bent towards numbers? Towards creativity? Do you excel in coaching? Speaking? Writing? What are those activities that when you do them, time flies by—you're in the zone! Your abilities are *not* just things that you're good at. They're activities that make you come alive when doing them.

Mike Miller is one of my great friends and another leader in our church. He leads a company called StrengthScope. The purpose of this company is to identify, leverage, and coach your key energizers in the workplace. It's an amazing concept. He has worked extensively with our church staff on this. Although StrengthScope is a corporate tool being used by companies like Facebook and Sony, it's really God's plan for each of us all along. When we operate in our spiritual giftedness as seen in Romans 12, 1 Corinthians 12, Ephesians 4, and 1 Peter 4, we start to come alive!

Knowing what makes you come alive and what drains you is key. Often times, we look at strengths and weaknesses from a traditional viewpoint. During an interview, if the interviewer asks you the standard question, "What are your strengths and weaknesses?" the answer that you'll probably give them is something like, "Well, I'm good at…" Well, if you're good at numbers but you *hate* doing them, does that strengthen or weaken you?

When you assess your abilities from God's perspective, you need to look deeper than merely where you

> **Don't ask yourself what the world needs. Ask yourself what makes you come alive, and go do that, because what the world needs is people who have come alive.**
> **—Howard Thurman**

excel. Ask yourself, "What makes me come alive?" Dr. Howard Thurman once told Gil Bailie, "Don't ask yourself what the world needs. Ask yourself what makes you come alive, and go do that, because what the world needs is people who have come alive."[7] The beauty of this is that when God stirs you with a Divine Disturbance, what makes you come alive will align exactly with what the world needs. It's a win-win.

God has wired you with a set of abilities and natural talents that you were born with. And when you gave your life to Christ, the Holy Spirit gave you at least one spiritual gift to help advance the cause of Christ in your generation. When these are working in harmony with each other, you'll never "work" a day in your life. It will be a calling. It will be your dream.

M: Maturity – *The "when" of your DREAM.*

Are you ready for the weight of God's dream for you? More than likely, you're not. The dream is ready, but *you're* not. I expand on this point in the next chapter on DELAY, but let me say this: while you think that you're waiting on God to fulfill his end of the bargain, he's waiting on *you* to prepare yourself.

I'll never forget the advice that one of my mentors, Dr. Don Fowler, professor and pastor, gave me one day regarding my future spouse. I was in college and recently dumped by my fiancée. I was devastated. I just *knew* that she was the one. But she tore out my heart and stomped on it one night when I caught her with her other boyfriend. Yeah, the *three* of us really didn't see eye-to-eye moving our marriage relationship forward together!

After a few months of feeling sorry for myself, I decided to get back in the dating game. But I was gun shy, as could be expected. That's when I barged into Dr. Fowler's small professor's office, books floor to ceiling, and said, "How do I know which girl is for me? How will I know? I don't want to make the wrong choice...*again.*"

He said, "Phil, here's your homework. Get a sheet of paper and write down all of the attributes and characteristics of your future spouse. Don't leave out any detail. Go to town. Keep in mind, these are the things you desire to see in *her* and no one else."

I went back to my dorm room and wrote about five pages of single-spaced lines on a yellow legal pad. I wrote everything I could think of. Godly. Funny. Passion for others. Selfless. Hard worker. Great family. Loves family. Great friend. I left out no detail.

When I arrogantly turned my stack of papers back to him, he took one glance at them and handed the legal pad back to me and said, "Phil, this is *your* list. Instead of focusing the someone else who meets this criteria, how about *you* determine to become your own dream list." Ouch. Although I had a dream, *I* was yet unready. I needed to mature. I needed to grow into the dream. So do you. Maybe God has yet to bless you with the fulfillment of his dream for you because you are still unready.

As you'll see in the next chapter, maybe you're lounging on the building block of DELAY.

MAKING IT REAL:

- Look back at the list comparing Fully Alive and Simply Breathing. Where do you fit? Why?

- Can you articulate your dream succinctly? If so, what is it? If not, have you considered a fast for vision clarity? What kind of fast are you going to do? When will you start? Record your progress.

- As you reflect on the five D.R.E.A.M filters, which one resonates most? Why?

Desire - *The "what" of your* DREAM.
Reason - *The "why" of your* DREAM.
Experiences - *The "who" of your* DREAM.
Abilities - *The "how" of your* DREAM.
Maturity - *The "when" of your* DREAM.

DELAY

DREAM

DEPENDENCE

DISTURBANCE

BUILDING BLOCK FOUR

Building Block 4:

DELAY

*The only thing worse than waiting on God
is wishing you would have waited on God.*

Unfortunately, one of my mottos is "Ready, FIRE, Aim." I don't like to wait. I'm guessing neither do you. My ninja-like grocery store checkout system proves this theory: Get your items. Make careful observation of the various checker-outers. Make mental notes of their speed, accuracy, posture, and competency. Scope the competition to see if grandma has her fanny pack full of coupons. Skip her line. Choose correctly. Complement the checker-outer on his mad skills *prior* to him scanning even one item. This is key. It builds confidence and turns him from good to great. Assist with the bagging. Pay. Head to the car while looking over my shoulder at the other pitiful folks still in line.

I won the bronze metal in this event back in the day. Trust me, my counselor says that I've come a long way!

Waiting in line is one thing.
Waiting in life is another.

As we follow the journey of Nehemiah, we see that he was DISTURBED over the condition of Israel and felt the birthing pains of a destiny being realized. He agonized in DEPENDENT prayer and fasting for several days which led him to clearly articulate his DREAM. Finally, he had it. His true north. His magnificent obsession had clarity and conviction. Not only did his DREAM close the gap between what could be and should be, but *now* he wanted to move to make it a reality.

Yet if you pay attention to the story, if you will dig in and read with alertness, you'll see a half-hidden gem.

> And it came to pass in the month of Nisan, in the twentieth year of King Artaxerxes, when wine was before him, that I took the wine and gave it to the king. Now I had never been sad in his presence before. Therefore the king said to me, "Why is your face sad, since you are not sick? This is nothing but sorrow of heart." (Nehemiah 2:1–2)

The king recognized something different about Nehemiah. The cupbearer was normally happy-go-lucky and cheerful in the king's presence. This time was different. This time, he was disturbed. To be sad before the king could have resulted in death. Yet, Nehemiah was willing to take that chance.

Before we dive into his conversation with the king, we need to focus on a critical and often overlooked part of the narrative. Notice what the text says: "It came to pass in the month of Nisan." According to the Jewish calendar the month of Nisan is four months from the time of Chislev, when Nehemiah's brother had given

Nehemiah had spent one third of a year contemplating the right opportunity for sharing his DREAM with anyone.

him the news about Jerusalem (1:1). Nehemiah had spent one third of a year contemplating the right opportunity for sharing his DREAM with anyone. Four, long, arduous months of wrestling with God in prayer and fasting. Four months of thinking about the dilapidated conditions of Jerusalem. Four months of being DISTURBED.

Although Nehemiah's passion lay poised for action like a coiled spring, he had to wait. As we see later in the story, Nehemiah was hardly a man who wanted to sit around and watch reruns. He was remarkably proactive. He wanted to *move*. He wanted to *act*. He *hated* to wait. But God knew that the best way for the DREAM to saturate his heart was to send him to the School of Delay.

THE SCHOOL OF DELAY

The School of Delay. Ugh. Even typing those words is difficult. But DELAY is God's plan. It has always been God's plan. Although the DREAM is real, it is yet unreal *in us*. Thus God enrolls our names into his famous school. In this school our patience will be tested and our perseverance maxed. Our heavenly schoolmaster registers us into classes like Loneliness 101, Failure 201, Frustration 301, and Bench Warming 401. God does this not out of hate. Quite the opposite. His motive is maturity. His method is DELAY.

I live in a suburb of Kansas City. I love everything about this city. It's home, and we're the absolute center of the United States. From the Kansas City International Airport, you can get anywhere, but, because it's not one of the major airports, we have to fly through other hubs to get to final destinations. For instance, recently my wife and I went to San Antonia via Chicago. On a map, Chicago is out of the way. But we had to go through Chicago on

It seems counterintuitive to fly backwards to fly forward.

the way to San Antonio. It seems counterintuitive to fly backwards to fly forward.

It's the same with God's School of Delay. Sometimes we have to go to Chicago and *wait* in order to get to San Antonio and *flourish*. You might be living in a spiritual Chicago and you're dreaming of San Antonio. Please know that God has you in Chicago because you might be yet unready for San Antonio.

GEMS FROM OSWALD

When I first became a Christ-follower at the age of sixteen, I started reading the daily devotional called *My Utmost For His Highest* by Oswald Chambers. These words are a powerful way to start your day.

Out of all of the daily gems in that book, two diamonds stood out to me among the rest. When I was a young, high school jock, these diamonds helped me gain a perspective on God's lifelong vision for me. These devotionals came at the perfect time amidst a summer of frustration. I needed clarity. I needed a dose of reality. These messages were just for me, springing forth on July 6 and July 28.

The first speaks of a valley between a vision and its move to reality. Without a vision made real in our own being, we are apt to fall to temptations and fail to complete it.

> God gives us the vision, then He takes us down to the valley [of humiliation] to batter us into the shape of the vision, and it is in the valley that so many of us faint and give way. . . . We are always in such a frantic hurry. In the light of the glory of the vision we go forth to do things, but the vision is not real in us yet; and God has to take us into the valley, and put us

through fires and floods to batter us into shape, until we get to the place where He can trust us with the veritable reality.

You might need to find a copy of Chamber's famous devotional—several authorized websites post the material online—and read the July 6 entry everyday as I once did. As I re-read it, I can't help but think about where you might be in your Divine Disturbance journey. You might be in the "valley of humiliation" today. You might have tried something and failed. Now, you feel the weight of people's scorn as they try to associate *you* with the project that went poorly or with an attempt less than great. But you have also adopted their wrong-minded association. You think that *you're* a failure because something that you did might have failed. Stop that thinking right now. *You* are not a failure. Yes, a project or ministry or book or job might have failed. Heck, it might have been a glorious failure! But that doesn't make *you* a failure. God might have needed to take you through the valley of humiliation to teach you this one lesson in his School of Delay.

> God has to take us into the valley, and put us through fires and floods to batter us into shape, until we get to the place where He can trust us.
> —Oswald Chambers

You might be going through the "fires and floods" that are "battering you into shape." Although you feel like a whipping boy tossed around in some cosmic chess game, you must realize that God is putting you through these fires and floods for your good and his glory (Romans 8:28). Like the child who sat on the floor looking up at his mother's cross-stitching thinking it was an absolute mess, it wasn't until he got up and saw the stitching from *her* view that it made sense. We are that child. We look up to the heavens and wonder why our lives are in such a mess. The tapestry threads run

When you can't trace the hand of God, you can trust the heart of God.

everywhere and make no sensible picture. From our perspective, our heavenly Father is nuts. However, from his perspective, he is working everything out according to his perfect plan. I've heard it said, "When you can't trace the hand of God, you can trust the heart of God."

Are you going to trust him when you are in the fires and floods?

Chambers makes another convicting point on July 6:

> Ever since we had the vision God has been at work, getting us into the shape of the ideal, and over and over again we escape from His hand and try to batter ourselves into our own shape.

Have you "escaped from His hand" and are now trying to "batter yourself into your own shape?" Many of us do that, don't we? We think that our way is better. Our way is faster. We don't need to wait. We justify our "Ready, FIRE, Aim" actions with excuses like, "I don't have time to wait!" "If I don't do this *now*, then it won't get done!" "I know that I'm not ready yet, but I'll learn as I go!"

HOW A THIRTY-SECOND CONVERSATION CHANGED MY PERSPECTIVE

I'll never forget the moment when this principle crystallized for me. I was seventeen years old. I had been a Christian for a whopping eight months and I knew all things Bible. Just ask me. I was charged and ready to change the world. I had my life's journey all paved out. Sixteen, get saved. Seventeen, learn. Eighteen, start a church. Nineteen, travel the world telling people how to build a mega-church. I had business cards printed, flyers made, and even a ministry pager.

(For those of you who don't know what a pager is, you've missed out on a great season of history).

All of my ministry plans came to a crashing halt one morning when some great friends of mine, Matt and Debbie Englebrake, took me to Einstein Brother's Coffee. I should have known something was up when the *parents* of my buddies were wanting to take me out to breakfast.

As we stood in line, Matt asked me about my ministry plans. I thought, heck yeah! Matt and Debbie want to join Team PMK to help launch this world-changing church next year! They're on board! They want to hear my vision and my strategy! So I started talking, and talking, and talking. I told him that I didn't need to go to Bible college or seminary because that would just waste time. I needed to start *now*.

We were still standing in line about to order when Matt asked me another question. "Okay, *pastor*," he said ("pastor" had a negative flare), "what are the Ten Commandments?"

"What?"

"You heard me."

"Umm, don't kill. Don't steal. Don't lie. Have no other God before me. Love your neighbor as yourself. No, wait. Umm. God helps those who help themselves...wait. No. Love Jesus?"

All the blood rushed from my face. I was completely and utterly embarrassed. My body started to go numb. The humiliation continued.

"Okay, *pastor*, where are the Ten Commandments *located*?"

"Umm. In the Old Testament."

"Is that all you got? The Old Testament? Don't you think you might need some training to add to your passion? Let's reconsider Bible college and seminary, what do you say?"

This entire conversation happened before we got our food. I knew what I needed to do. I'm thankful for various people who told me what I *needed* to hear instead of what I *wanted* to hear. What about you? Who are you listening to?

OSWALD GEM 2.0

After about a month of being *rocked* by Chamber's July 6 soul bomb, the July 28 torpedoed my dreams. I opened the devotional and read these words:

> We are apt to imagine that if Jesus Christ constrains us, and we obey Him, He will lead us to great success. We must never put our dreams of success as God's purpose for us; His purpose may be exactly the opposite. We have an idea that God is leading us to a particular end, a desired goal; He is not. The question of getting to a particular end is a mere incident. What we call the process, God calls the end.

Over and over, Chambers' daggers pierced my soul and still give me perspective today: "What we call the process, God calls the end. . . . It is the process, not the end, which is glorifying to God. . . . What men call training and preparation, God calls the end." When I think about these words, I often draw a simple line with two points. Left point is where I am now. Right point is several inches above the left; it's my goal. Then under it I draw another line with two points.

What we call the process, God calls the end.
—Oswald Chambers

This one, however, looks more like the stock market. Ups. Downs. Peaks. Valleys. Plateaus. This is reality. Our view of success and God's view of success is measured by the two contrasting lines.

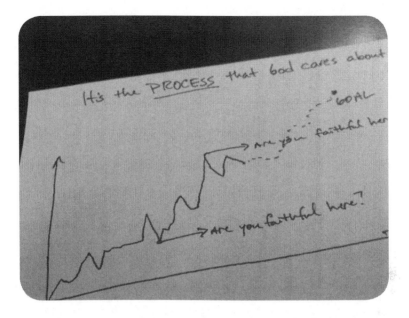

We often point to the line that goes up and to the right with no resistance as God's favor and his will. In our warped view of reality, we feel that God, because he loves us, wants us always to succeed. Remember back to chapter two—your view is skewed. Your view of God dictates your actions and your view of success. You probably view him as a genie in a bottle, at your every beck and call.

Ups. Downs. Peaks. Valleys. Plateaus. These are all tools in the Master's toolbox to prune us and shape us more into his image. It is in the valley where the dream of God is made real. And God looks at you and me in the *midst* of the School of Delay, where his fires and floods seem at their peak, and says, "This is my boy! This is my girl! They have made it! Look how they handled that problem! Look how their attitude is! Look how they reflect my Son's image onto everyone around them! Even though they *think* that they haven't met their goal yet, even though they *think* that they're a long ways off, to me, they have already reached it!"

The process is the goal. Whew.

OBSESSED WITH PERFECTION

Maybe this principle means more to me than most because of the way I grew up. From birth to age seven, I lived every boy's dream. My parents, Mike and Joann, and my two older sisters, Pam and Michelle, and I all lived on a few acres in the "sticks" of Spring Hill, Kansas. Growing up, Spring Hill had a population of twenty-five hundred people (that's counting pregnant women twice). My daily routine was to hop on my bike and ride wherever the wind took me. Nirvana. Utopia. Wonderful. *Ignorant.*

The *reality* of the situation was that my dad was a drunk. His morning routine was coffee and a screwdriver (vodka and orange juice). When he wasn't drinking, he was the nicest guy on the planet. He never met a stranger. But those times when he *wasn't* drinking were few and far between. As a kid, I thought that every dad took two-hour naps on the baseball bleachers during a tournament. I thought that it was normal for other kid's parents to take you home because dad was passed out at the school recital.

That's why it shocked me when, at age seven, my mom informed me that she was divorcing my dad. I was devastated. Again, I was ignorant.

I'll never forget sitting in Mrs. Wills' first grade classroom at Spring Hill Elementary the day it finally hit home to me that my parents were calling it quits. To every other kid there, it was a normal day of fun, learning, and recess. To me, my world had just ended.

Once I caught my breath, I remember telling her these words, "My parents are getting a divorce. *And it's my fault."*

I sat at my desk and tried to hold back the tears. They started coming like a hurricane. But I was the fastest kid in my grade. I had a rep to keep. I couldn't show emotion. So, I held it in as long as

I could—for 4.2 seconds. Then it all came out. The ugly cry. Snot. Hyperventilation. Tears. Repeat. I tried to hide it by opening up the top of my old school desk and sticking my head in where my crayons were stored. I wasn't fooling anyone. Especially Mrs. Wills.

She took me by the hand, walked me to the hallway, knelt down, and embraced me as if it were an airport reunion. Her shoulder was my refuge. When I came up for air, she asked me what was wrong. Once I caught my breath, I remember telling her these words, "My parents are getting a divorce. *And it's my fault.*"

I knew it was my fault. I wasn't a good enough son. I was a failure as a brother. I made an error at my recent baseball game. I didn't do well enough on my spelling test. And so it began.

I blamed myself. So, in order to fix that which was broken, I needed to do better. Better grades. Better performance. Better results. More championships. More trophies. As a kid, I was driven. Obsessed with perfection.

WIN OR DIE TRYING

When I got older and realized the truth behind my parents' divide, I already had a preprogrammed mental state of win or die trying. To make matters worse, my dad, who now lived only twenty minutes away and whom I visited every other weekend, would come to every game with a video camera in one hand and a hidden flask in the other.

The game would always *begin* with nice words from the bleachers. But then, as the innings progressed, so did the liquid. If I hit a single, he would shout, "Should have been a double!" If I got four hits out of five times at the plate, I was scolded for the one strikeout. If I threw three touchdowns but one interception, you guessed it—focus on the interception. Repeat this cycle and just insert a sport or

Maybe you are the person stuck on the hamster wheel of production for affection.

academics of your choice. Magnify it when induced by alcohol.

Once you understand that warped view of success was my backdrop, you can see why this "July 28" moment from *My Utmost for His Highest* came as such a welcomed friend. "What we call the process, God calls the end" gave me permission to try and fail. If the goal wasn't always what I produced, but rather the character of my heart and the discipline in the process, I didn't have to set so many unrealistic expectations on myself. Consequently, I realized that my *heavenly* Father loved me unconditionally, with no prerequisite of an ability to produce.

Maybe you are the person stuck on the hamster wheel of production for affection. In your mind, you believe that unless you produce *for* God, you won't receive love *from* God. In doing so, you're suffering from what I call the Eclipse Syndrome: when your work *for* God overshadows your relationship *with* God. You've become a Martha instead of a Mary (see Luke 10:38–42). You have become a slave, held in bondage to results.

A better way whispers your name. Others have answered the call. Will you?

MEET YOUR CLASSMATES IN THE SCHOOL OF DELAY

There's good news and bad news in God's School of Delay. The bad news is that enrolling in this school is a prerequisite for fulfilling your God-birthed dream. The good news is that you have lots of other classmates on the journey with you. Even after a cursory reading of the Bible, you see that you are not alone. Let's look at a few of your classmates.

Noah

God told Noah to prepare for a pending judgment on mankind by building the ark. Check. Noah went out to fulfill God's command by getting wood. Check. Tools. Check. Divine blue print. Check. Noah had caught God's dream and was eager to complete it! Yet do you know how long it took Noah to complete the ark? Anywhere between sixty and 120 years! That detail was written nowhere on his task list. Talk about being enrolled in the School of Delay!

I'm sure the excitement of partnering with God to help give humanity a second chance wore off about the second year into the gig. Maybe sooner than that. But while Noah was building the ark, God was building Noah's heart. God was chiseling away at Noah's character so that he and his family could handle the weight of being solely responsible for replenishing the earth! Talk about a world-changing mission! Here's the key—usually the larger the scope of God's dream, the longer you're enrolled in the School of Delay.

Joseph

Imagine that you're the second youngest of twelve boys in the family, and you receive a dream from God that all other brothers will bow down to you in submission one day. Yeah, I think that an old-fashioned, middle school swirly would be on cue for you. That's what happened to Joseph. Everyone already knew that Joseph was Daddy's favorite. Now this was the icing on the cake. Instead of getting a swirly, though, Joseph spent the next thirteen years either as a slave or in prison. Why? Because although he had the coat of many colors, God knew that he didn't need a coat, but rather character.

If you look at Joseph's story closely, you'll see that God's hand of favor and providence was with him every step of the way. God knew what he was doing. He was preparing Joseph for greatness by allowing him to be refined in isolation and pruned in patience. I'm sure that Joseph felt the angst of having a DREAM, a vision of what could and should be, only to be sitting in prison, falsely accused of a crime that he never committed, thinking the entire time, "Where is God? Why would he allow this? Does he *not* know what he's doing?"

Joseph was just a punk kid who caught the wave of God's dream. That one DREAM set his trajectory. But in God's economy, the way up is down. To go up, you must dig deep. Little did he know that God's upward movement meant going from the pit, to Potiphar's house, to prison, and *finally* to the palace. These thirteen years in supposed obscurity *re*fined Joseph's character instead of *de*fining him by his circumstances (more on this later).

Abraham

God gave Abraham the DREAM of Promised Land, Promised People, and Promised Blessing. This came in Genesis 12 in what's traditionally called the Abrahamic Covenant. Our heavenly Father made a promise with the seventy-five-year-old Abraham and said that all this was going to come through his lineage.

One slight problem. Abraham was seventy-five years old and still without child. But Abraham was a man of faith, and he believed God. As the years passed, his initial excitement faded. Months went by. Nothing. Years went by. Nothing. Decades went by. Still nothing.

You cannot fulfill a legitimate DREAM through illegitimate decisions.

Finally, when Abraham was ninety-nine years old and his wife was ninety, the Angel of the Lord paid them a special visit and reiterated the DREAM that God had for them. When Sarah heard these words, she laughed. They both chuckled in their spirits because the thought of having children at such an old age. Nevertheless, God remained true to his promise for them and they gave birth to Isaac, whose name means, "Son of Laughter."

This would be a wonderful story, had not Abraham and Sarah, a few years into receiving God's dream (and a few years *before* Isaac was born), gotten impatient and tried to manufacture God's timetable. Even though God had promised a son between *them*, they hurried the process. Regardless of the external pressures that the couple was facing, they determined to jump ahead of God and take matters into their own hands. Abraham slept with his maidservant Haggar, and she gave birth to Ishmael. Ishmael was *not* the son of Promise. Consequently, the entire divide between Christianity and Islam stems from this major distinction. The Islamic faith believes that Ishmael was God's chosen seed, *not* Isaac. Ugh. Remember, the only thing worse than waiting on God is wishing that you had!

What does this have to do with *your* DREAM? Everything. When you hijack God's providential process of pruning and try to accomplish his dream your way, you'll cause more damage than you'll ever know. You cannot fulfill a legitimate DREAM through illegitimate decisions. Regardless of how fast you feel you need to go, if it's not on God's timetable and according to God's standards, it's not God's way. There are no shortcuts to fulfilling your God-birthed dream. Sometimes what seems like a detour is actually God's superhighway. You don't see it at the time, but God is orchestrating everything according to his plan. Do you trust him?

Moses

Imagine what it would be like if you were raised for greatness in the lap of luxury, groomed with the world's finest education, poised to walk into your father's footsteps as the next great ruler of the world only to wake up one day and realize that you are not who you thought you were. You were adopted. And the slaves on whose shoulders the economic burden for your entire empire rests are *your* people, *your* family, *your* heritage, *your* identity.

This was Moses' life. When he turned forty, many scholars believe, he discovered his true identity. Maybe he had never heard the amazing story of his upbringing. Maybe he thought he was actually Pharaoh's next in line. Regardless of what he *knew*, we know what he *did*. He became DISTURBED over the condition of his people. This was his moment. This was when the brutal facts of reality *rocked* his world. This is when God implanted him with a Divine Disturbance. It started a fire in his soul that couldn't be extinguished. He couldn't bear the thought that Pharaoh (his "dad") was cruelly building his empire on the backs of Moses' own bloodline.

Although it's great to start with DISTURBANCE, unhindered and reckless disturbance will create more damage than good. Moses caught a vision for delivering his people, God's people, from this bondage. But instead of waiting on God to show the next steps, Moses took matters into his own hands. Literally.

He went out and found the first slave master he saw, killed him, and buried him under the sand (like a good mafia movie). Moses had a legitimate DREAM—to deliver the people. He went about it by making illegitimate decisions—killing off people singlehandedly.

The DISTURBANCE was real. The DREAM was real. But they were *yet unreal in Moses*. That's when God had to enroll Moses in the School of Delay.

When word spread about Moses' actions, he became a fugitive and ran as far and fast as he could go. He met a girl whose father was a shepherd. They got married, and Moses started working for his father-in-law. Talk about humbling! There is nothing wrong with working for your father-in-law. There is nothing wrong with being a shepherd. But when you have been groomed to rule the world, hanging out with sheep in an obscure land, totally disconnected from society isn't exactly your dream job. Moses was in Chicago.

But God was up to something BIG. And the bigger the DREAM, the longer the DELAY. It is in the School of Delay where the DREAM has time to marinate. If you are in the School of Delay, maybe you are thinking that you are waiting on God. Perhaps God is waiting on you.

Moses had no plans of going back to Egypt. That's why he spent the next forty years as a shepherd. Imagine spending forty years with a burning passion to do something for God and not being allowed to carry it through! Unbeknownst to Moses, God was working out the details behind the scenes to use this now seasoned dreamer to change the world.

WAITING 2.0

I could go on and on listing examples of men and women in the Bible who had to enroll in God's School of Delay. **Joshua** had to sit as Moses' back-up quarterback for forty years. And yet even after such amazing grooming, God still had to get up in his face and give him the pre-game pep talk, saying three times, "Be strong and courageous!"

Paul, after receiving the DREAM to preach the gospel to the Gentiles, had to spend three years on the backside of the desert in Arabia receiving special revelation. These years were spent in isolation and obscurity. Why? Was he on a detour? Absolutely not. He was being chiseled into the leader and preacher God wanted him to be.

What about **Jesus**? Imagine coming down from heaven, being born as a peasant, spending thirty years as a carpenter, running the family business, knowing all the while that you are pulling off the greatest *Undercover Boss* episode in history! Jesus enrolled in God's School of Delay as well. Thirty years in relative obscurity. Thirty years communing with his heavenly Father before his public ministry began. Thirty years of waiting. If *you* are waiting, take heart. Jesus can empathize with you! Maybe that gives new light to Hebrews 4:15–16 that says:

> For we do not have a High Priest who cannot sympathize with our weaknesses, but was in all points tempted as we are, yet without sin. Let us therefore come boldly to the throne of grace, that we may obtain mercy and find grace to help in time of need.

Was he tempted to quit? Yep. Was he tempted to take a shortcut? Absolutely. Was he tempted to live a comfortable life and not fulfill his heavenly Father's will? You bet. But he followed through to the very end. "Therefore," Hebrews says, "We can come boldly to the throne of grace"!

I have been a student *of* the School of Delay as well as being a student *in* the School of Delay. Every time I hear someone share their story of God doing something great through them, my ears perk up at the points when they discuss dark periods of seeming inactivity or inaction. These are points along the journey when they feel stuck. They're in a rut (remember the only difference between a rut and a grave is its depth).

You'll never fulfill all that God has for you by being held hostage by labels.

The thing that separates the stories of greatness and the stories of mediocrity is always this one factor: Were they *de*fined by their DELAY or *re*fined by it? Let me explain.

DEFINED BY DELAY

Labels are powerful. They can be the catalyst that drives you onward or they can be the noose that pulls you downward. When faced with failure, frustration, or fatigue, our enemy Satan does a masterful job of reaching inside of our minds and causing us to label ourselves.

Here are some common labels that I've heard:

"I'm just a divorced parent."

"I'm an addict and can't help anyone."

"I'm such a failure."

"I'm a loser. I've always been a loser and will always be a loser."

These are more than self-fulfilling prophecies. These labels are causing people to remain sundials in the shade. You'll never fulfill all that God has for you by being held hostage by labels. In essence, you are letting your circumstance or situation define you. Here's when you know you're being defined by your situation: you've substituted a *project label* with a *personal legacy*.

Project Label = *a temporary project that worked other than you intended*

Personal Legacy = *how you will be remembered and your impact on others*

Instead of saying, "Oh, the project didn't work out this time and failed," you say, "Oh, I *never* can get things to work out and I'm such a *failure*." See what just happened? It's a small tweak in your vocabulary and in your mindset, but it makes a huge difference. In fact, maybe the breakthrough you've been waiting for will happen when you change one letter—change *d* to *r*.

REFINED BY DELAY

There's a better way to look at DELAY. Instead of being *de*fined by it, choose to be *re*fined by it. When you do this, you change the script. You move past the immediate. You catch a vision for *why* God is putting you on this holding pattern. Instead of blaming your past, you're framing your future.

- Maybe you're unready to handle the weight of God's dream for your life.

- Maybe there are some things in your life that need to be chiseled out by the master sculptor.

- Maybe God needs to teach you some private lessons before you have a public launch.

- Maybe God wants you to humble yourself privately now to avoid having to humiliate you publicly later.

When you are refined by your DELAY (or failure or setback), you are like the silversmith who is molding silver over a burning fire. How does the silversmith know when the silver is just right? When he takes the silver out of the fire, looks at it, and can see his reflection in silver. All of the impurities have burned out. The fire has produced perfection.

In the same way, our Savior might be holding you out over the fire so that, when you are finished, he can pull you out and see *his* reflection in you.

ARE YOU IN THE DESERT?

I love what Charles Swindoll says about the desert experiences of our lives. He writes:

> Once God finds the desert that you need, He ushers you off the bus and drives away. At least it seems that way. And the instant feeling you get is, God's gone. Where is He? He's left me in this place! In the midst of this painful experience, you find you are no longer able to do things you once were able to do. Fear sets in. You say to yourself, I'm going to lose my gifts. I'm going to lose my usefulness. I'm forgotten. God's left me behind. Time is running out. Opportunities are passing my by. I'll never get out of this place.[8]

If you feel like you are on the backside of the desert, in the wilderness of wasteland, you're blessed. God might have you right where he wants you. Remember when the Hebrew people, through the leadership of Moses, crossed the Red Sea on dry ground and entered the brink of their Promised Land? After crossing the sea, a mere eleven-day journey lay between them and their Promised Land. Only eleven days. But they had a penchant for stretching an eleven-day journey into forty years of wandering in circles. Apparently they lacked a GPS!

Actually, they traveled in circles due to their lack of faith. When

If you feel like you are on the backside of the desert, in the wilderness of wasteland, you're blessed. God might have you right where he wants you.

their spies came back from inspecting this new land, ten out of twelve shook with fear. Consequently, God said that the entire adult generation that had crossed the sea would die off, and the younger generation would inherit the land instead.

God established the new plan with this command: Follow the pillar of cloud by daytime and the pillar of smoke at night. If the cloud moved to the right, move the camp to the right. If the fire and smoke moved left, then move the camp left. Pretty simple. Well, that fire and smoke caused the Hebrews to wander in circles for the next forty years! As you can imagine, the followers got pretty upset. They became incredibly angry with Moses, their leader, and they became resentful of God himself. Not only were they traveling seemingly *nowhere*, but also everyone over twenty years old started dying. I'm not talking about a few funerals a year. I'm talking about 137 funerals a day! Every day. For forty years. The wasteland became a massive graveyard.

They thought that God had abandoned them. That their heavenly Father had neglected them. That he had taken his eye off of them. Quite the opposite was true. One of the most comforting verses in the Bible highlights this very point.

> "He found him [Israel] in a desert land,
> And in the howling waste of a wilderness;
> He **encircled** him, He **cared** for him,
> He **guarded** him as the **pupil of His eye**.
> "Like an eagle that stirs up its nest,
> That hovers over its young,
> He spread His wings and caught them,
> He carried them on His pinions.
> The Lord alone **guided** him." (Deuteronomy 32:10–12a; NASB; emphasis mine)

In the midst of Israel's frustration about being in the wilderness (their School of Delay), God was caring for them. He encircled them. He guided them. He guarded them. How did God guard them? *As the pupil of his eye!* Let me ask you this. What is one of the most protected parts of your body? Besides the groin area for men, it's the pupil of your eye. You don't let anything or anyone touch it. Why? Because even the smallest speck of dust landing in your eye can cause serious damage.

Here's the point. When you are in God's School of Delay, when you think that you're in the wilderness, take heart. You are being protected as the pupil of God's eye. He is not going to let anything happen to you that is outside of his will. Rest in this.

God wants us to be faithful in the midst of DELAY. Nehemiah had massive amounts of leadership and organization in his bones. And yet he was a glorified waiter. I'm sure that for years he dreamed of using those gifts and abilities to do something great. Little did he know that God was working everything according to his perfect plan. But what if Nehemiah had proved unfaithful *while* he was waiting? What if he had arrived late to meetings, slept in, half-heartedly accomplished his duties, and gossiped among the staff? God might never have trusted him with the weight of his *real* purpose, and we wouldn't be reading about him thousands of years later!

> **He is not going to let anything happen to you that is outside of his will. Rest in this.**

Bloom where you're planted. Grow where you are. Quit daydreaming about the greener grass someday. Start watering your own yard today.

WASHING WHILE WAITING

I look forward every few months to our church's quarterly men's breakfasts. I'm amazed each time when I see over 150 men show up at 6:45 a.m. to eat together, challenge one another, and (usually) listen to a great speaker.

When we invited Jeff Martin, a Vice President of the Fellowship of Christian Athletes, to come and speak, I had no idea what I was in for. His fabulous talk was titled "The Aggressive Pursuit of Rest." His points were spot on, and his closing illustration connected with *every* man in the room. You could hear a pin drop.

All Jeff wanted to do was be a pastor—shepherd God's flock. The Divine Disturbance that God burned on his heart while a teenager was to take care of God's "sheep," his people. When Jeff enrolled in seminary, he had visions of grandeur. He dreamed of preaching, teaching, and leading a group of people from where they were to where God wanted them to be. It was his magnificent obsession.

But things didn't work out the way he wanted. All Jeff's buddies began getting ministry jobs, traveling, preaching, teaching, and being greatly used by God. What was Jeff doing? Washing the campus maintenance trucks in the shipping and receiving dock. Day in and day out, Jeff was stuck with a spray wand and a bucket of soap. To make matters worse, most of his buddies who were traveling and speaking on the weekends would use these trucks to haul various equipment (speakers, band gear, tables, etc.). Everything inside of him wanted to be "out there" doing real ministry. He wanted to skip class in the School of Delay and never reenroll.

Jeff's entire perspective changed one day when he read the various Old Testament passages that spoke of David being a shepherd. He was out in the fields, in complete isolation, tending sheep. The future king of Israel was refining his faith in the crucible of loneliness. When a bear or lion would come up and attack his precious sheep, he would exercise extreme amounts of faith and kill the bear or lion (see 1 Samuel 17:34–35).

All of this was rolling through Jeff's mind as he washed the same trucks that he had scrubbed a million times before. And then it hit him like a ton of bricks. He looked at these trucks and he saw not maintenance trucks, but sheep. White tops. Black tires. All huddled together. Dripping wet after a fresh bathing. Looking straight at their faithful shepherd who diligently had been cleaning them every night. Faithful. In isolation. But faithful.

> **He looked and saw not maintenance trucks, but sheep. White tops. Black tires. All huddled together. Dripping wet after a fresh bathing.**

Jeff said, "God had put me in charge of my flock. It was the answer to my prayers. I just didn't see it. I was tending the flock that he gave me, and God built into my soul the character for taking care of his *real* flock one day!" He had to get his master's degree in the School of Delay. What about you?

Instead of becoming jaded and bitter at God for making your DELAY seem so long, be grateful for this season of pruning, refining, and molding. It is the process not the end that concerns God. Change your script. Turn your loneliness into a lesson, your test into a testimony, and your mess into a message. When God is through with you in his School of Delay, you'll be ready to carry the weight of what's coming next.

MAKING IT REAL:

- What stood out to you as your read the two devotionals from Oswald Chambers? Why do you think it impacted you the way it did?

- What are some lessons that you've learned in the School of Delay?

- How can you allow your School of Delay to *re*fine you instead of *de*fine you?

- Let's say your Divine Disturbance is fulfilled today, would you honestly be able to handle its magnitude? Why or why not?

- Have you thanked God for your season of waiting? If not, do so now.

DECLARE

DELAY

DREAM

DEPENDENCE

DISTURBANCE

BUILDING BLOCK FIVE

Building Block 5:

DECLARE

In a noisy world, everyone is speaking. Few are communicating.

I used to have a sttu...ssttuut...stuttering problem. Sometimes it still creeps up on me in awkward moments while I'm preaching in front of hundreds of people. Yeah, it's awful. It's as if my brain locks and I can't get the words out. I get stuck on a section of a word, and it jams in my mouth.

This problem was especially difficult as a high school quarterback. Imagine this scene. It's the fourth quarter. We're running the two-minute drill and marching down the field. It's a critical third down. I'm in the huddle looking at all of my teammates. I'm their leader. They're looking to me for confident leadership. We're all sweaty, bloody, and exhausted. I look over to the sidelines to see the play. Got it. Now, I open my mouth to give them precise direction for the next play. Only my brain has gone on strike.

"Okay, we got this one, guys! Listen up. Trips right, th...th... th...thir...thirty...thrrree..."

The play clock is counting down. Time is running out.

Not now. No. Seriously! Speak, Phil!

"Trips right, th...th...thirt...thirty three half ba...ba...back lead option...j...j...jet. On two, on two. Ready, break."

A lifetime passed during those few seconds of awkwardness. It was painful.

Here's the crazy thing about stuttering. Did you know that you cannot stutter when you sing? For some reason, when you sing, you use a different part of your brain, and words come out smooth as silk. So, you can imagine how uncool it might have seemed when I was calling the plays in the huddle and sometimes I would break out into a song! Hey, a man's gotta do what a man's gotta do!

It's one thing to stutter when trying to call a play.

It's another thing to stutter when trying to communicate your Divine Disturbance.

I am mesmerized with great communicators. I read everything I can get my hands on regarding communication. I study presidents, preachers, motivational speakers, athletes giving post-game interviews, ancient speeches, TED talks, office chatter, and even comedians.

Leverage the principles of great communication to work in your favor as you begin to share your Divine Disturbance.

What separates the *great* talks from *good* talks? How can some people rally groups of people around a common vision they might not even agree with while others can't seem to convince someone to run out of a burning building? More importantly, how can *you* leverage the principles of great communication to work in your favor as you begin to share your Divine Disturbance?

RESETTING THE BACKDROP

Let's remember where we've been. First, Nehemiah gets word about the dilapidated condition of Jerusalem, and he becomes DISTURBED. Although he's disturbed over the fact that God's people living in God's city are improperly protected, the *main* reason why he's so upset is that God's people aren't living up to their potential. They are missing out on God's best. And it's not *their* reputation on the line, it's their heavenly Father's. And Nehemiah has had enough.

Next, not quite knowing exactly *what* to do about the situation, Nehemiah climbs the next building block in the journey. He bathes it in DEPENDENCE—dependent prayer. He confesses his sins and reminds God of his character and covenant. This is not a one-time prayer, though. Day in, day out. He consistently makes courageous requests.

After the first two building blocks are built into the foundation of his soul, a DREAM starts to bud. He starts envisioning a better future for God's people. The tension between what currently *is* and what *could be* drives him. While still performing his butler duties, this cupbearer is fueled with a desire (the what), a reason (the why), the experience (the who), the abilities (the how) and the maturity (the when) of his DREAM.

But he's not ready yet. And neither is the world. His DREAM has to marinate. Mature. Grow up. So God enrolls him into the School of Delay. Both the dreamer and the dream are forced to either be refined in the crucible of DELAY or be defined by the crux of the desert.

And after four arduous months of waiting in seeming silence, Nehemiah finally gets his opportunity to share his Divine Disturbance.

How does he break the news to his boss? How does he cast the vision to those who would eventually rebuild the wall? Does he stutt…stt…stuutter? Does he search for the right words? Let's find out!

PRIVATE DECLARATION

The first step in DECLARING your Divine Disturbance is to be able to do this privately. You can't communicate your Divine Disturbance to the masses until you first learn to share it with those closest to you. It's what I call the Napkin Test. Can you articulate this God-birthed dream with someone else while sitting across a coffee shop table and all you have is a napkin? You might have to draw it in a picture or make bullet points. All you have is one napkin. That's what Nehemiah had to do.

> And it came to pass…when wine was before [King Artaxerxes], that I took the wine and gave it to the king. Now I had never been sad in his presence before. Therefore the king said to me, "Why is your face sad, since you are not sick? This is nothing but sorrow of heart."
> So I became dreadfully afraid, and said to the king, "May the king live forever! Why should my face not be sad, when the city, the place of my fathers' tombs, lies waste, and its gates are burned with fire?" (Nehemiah 2:1–3)

Nehemiah's DISTURBANCE was obvious. He couldn't contain it anymore. It had reached a boiling point. And those closest to him couldn't help but notice. Wisely, the king also noticed that this was not just a regular sadness. This was a broken heart, a Divine

Disturbance. So, when the king asked what was the matter, Nehemiah had his chance. I'm sure that he had been praying about this chance for some time. All of a sudden it arrived. He must have thought, *Here goes nothing!*

> **Can you articulate this God-birthed dream with someone else while sitting across a coffee shop table and all you have is a napkin?**

Notice that he was initially "dreadfully afraid." I find that comforting. He had the butterflies that we all do. His heart skipped. His palms were sweaty. His face flushed. Remember, his attitude change before the king could have resulted in immediate death. Yet, like all dreamers who desire to take their God-birthed dream from the sidelines to the field, he opened his mouth.

In the context of sharing his DREAM, Nehemiah showed honor and respect by saying, "May the king live forever." He didn't assume anything. He recognized the value of the person in front of him and created a sense of safety with his humility. This is key. Even though we might have an audacious, world-changing, earth-shattering kind of dream, we don't want to come across as a know-it-all or some arrogant jerk. Whoever we're with, we must show respect and humility.

THE *WHY* BEHIND THE *WHAT*
(Lead with the Burden)

In starting to communicate his Divine Disturbance, he begins with the *why* behind the *what*. People don't care *what* you're dreaming of doing until they first understand *why* you want to do it. What's the reason (remember, we talked about this in chapter three)? Why is this so important to you? Why do you feel so compelled to pursue it? What's your motivation behind such an audacious request?

People don't care *what* you're dreaming of doing until they first understand *why* you want to do it.

Keep in mind, people can sniff a fake from a mile away. They can tell if you are in the game for selfish greed or empty glory. You're not fooling anyone. But if your *why* is pure and God-glorifying, then continue communicating it. If not, retreat back to building block number one and beg God to, once again, break your heart for what breaks his. And guess what, God's heart breaks over pride! Ouch.

Nehemiah told the *why* convincingly. He didn't mince words. He didn't try to be politically correct or overly positive. He didn't say, "Well, Mr. King, the reason why I'm a little quiet today is because Jerusalem needs an economic turnaround and more protection." No! In the same way he received the brutal facts of reality, he *gave* the brutal facts. He said, "Why should my face *not* be sad?" Boom. He couldn't help but grieve. He couldn't help but be moved. And he brought the king into the mix.

In answering the king's question, Nehemiah, as was customary for Jewish rabbis to do, answered a question with a question. Instead of going straight into outlining his plans, Nehemiah piqued the king's curiosity and heightened his sympathy with a question about why he shouldn't feel sad about the condition of his forefather's graves. As Warren Wiersbe writes, "To Nehemiah, the past was a rudder to guide him and not an anchor to hold him back."[9]

Nehemiah then laid it out in plain language and gave the *why*. This was the real motivation. This was the heart. He said, in essence, "The city of my ancestors—my people— my heritage— is in complete shambles, ruined from the ground up, and its gates and walls have been burned and utterly destroyed." What he didn't say, but surely implied, was that Persia benefitted from Jerusalem being in such a pitiful condition. And who was leading the Persian movement? You guessed it, King Artaxerxes, the very man with whom Nehemiah was speaking (not to mention the very man that was his boss and who held the keys in the palm of his hand to Nehemiah's continued life). But when a man is fueled by God's courage through dependent prayer, even the world's most influential person lacks enough intimidation to affect him!

> **When a man is fueled by God's courage through dependent prayer, even the world's most influential person lacks enough intimidation to affect him!**

THE *WHAT* BEHIND THE *WHY*
(Follow with Details)

You need more than merely a compelling reason to make change. Otherwise, you'll be merely another daydreamer with a wish. No. A Divine Disturbance is more than a wish. It's a must—with a plan. It's a moral imperative that connects the dots between what currently *is* and what *should be*. It's something that must happen, *and you know how*. In other words, you have considered the details.

After hearing Nehemiah's *why*, the king asked him one of the most powerful questions anyone can ask. This was the point where Nehemiah's DISTURBANCE and DEPENDENCE collided.

"What do you request?" was the king's simple question (2:4). It may seem simple, but it was pregnant with implication. When the most powerful man in the world asks you "What do you request?" you'd better have a plan. You can't fudge this one. There's no "fake it till you make it" here. You either have a plan or you don't. You've either thought it through or you haven't.

Thankfully, our hero did have a plan. Or else his book would be a depressing story of hype. What if, when the king asked Nehemiah

that question, Nehemiah responded with, "I don't really know...
but somebody needs to do something about that!" Or he could have
tucked his DREAM under the rug of safety and said, "I request that we *pray* for my hometown...that someone rebuilds its walls." That would have

A Divine Disturbance is more than a wish. It's a must—with a plan.

been a tragedy of magnificent proportions.

No, when asked the question, Nehemiah had done enough research and preparation so that he could give an honest account to the king (2:6). Remember, he had spent the previous four months strategizing and dreaming on paper. You might have a good idea, but it's not a God-idea until it's written down. You must have a plan.

God echoed a similar truth to the prophet Habakkuk. Let these words rattle in your mind and sink into your soul. God commanded the prophet:

> "Write the vision and make it plain on tablets,
> That he may run who reads it.
> For the vision is yet for an appointed time;
> But at the end it will speak, and it will not lie.
> Though it tarries, wait for it;
> Because it will surely come,
> It will not tarry." (Habakkuk 2:2–3)

It doesn't get much clearer than that. "Write the vision and make it plain on tablets." Why do we need to take the time to write down the vision, the dream? In Habakkuk's case, the Lord wanted the prophet to write down the vision so that people would run *from* it. That might be your strategy. You want people to run *from* a certain lifestyle or situation. Or you might write down your Divine Disturbance so someone else has the opportunity to run *with* it. People don't run from or with a fuzzy vision. They don't tell their friends about obscure concepts. You can't motivate a tribe with vague generalities. Remember Marcus Buckingham's phrase, "Clarity is the antidote to anxiety."[10] When you are clear, it allows others to rally for your cause and about your cause.

> **You can't motivate a tribe with vague generalities.**

Nehemiah was exuberantly clear about his mission and his method. We've already looked at his *mission* (rebuilding Jerusalem's walls so God's fame could once again reign in his city and so God's people could live according to his Word). Now let's look at the *method* Nehemiah articulated.

He was extremely clear about what he needed from the king.

LETTERS. LUMBER. LIVES.

Nehemiah's request required more than the king's passive permission. It required the king's active participation because King Artaxerxes held control over three items that Nehemiah needed for a successful mission. No wonder Nehemiah prayed for favor in his presence!

Letters

> "Let letters be given to me for the governors of the region beyond the River, that they must permit me to pass through till I come to Judah…" (Nehemiah 2:7)

On the nine-hundred-mile (three to five month) journey from Persia to Jerusalem, Nehemiah knew he would encounter enormous amounts of adversity and protocol even *before* stepping foot onto

Jerusalem soil. If this Divine Disturbance were ever going to be realized, he would need some help. He needed letters that permitted him to make passage through the various territories and villages. Without these letters from the king, there would be no rebuilding effort.

Lumber

"...and a letter to Asaph the keeper of the king's forest, that he must give me timber to make beams for the gates of the citadel which pertains to the temple, for the city wall, and for the house that I will occupy." (2:8)

Lumber in Nehemiah's day was a scarce commodity, and forests were guarded carefully. Cutting wood without permission could put you before court or even to death. Therefore, it was essential that Nehemiah had permission to excavate entire sections of these forests!

Lives

Now the king had sent captains of the army and horsemen with me. (2:9)

It's interesting that when Nehemiah clearly communicated his Divine Disturbance to the king and boldly requested the letters and lumber, the king's heart was moved in such a way as to go beyond the call of duty. The king, understanding the reality of the situation at hand, released a military convoy to accompany Nehemiah. There was *no* way that Nehemiah could have been successful without all of the extra men accompanying him. You've got to be kidding me! Talk about the favor of God!

Why did the king do this? It was not just one thing. It was the culmination of Nehemiah's DISTURBANCE, fueled by DEPENDENT prayer, which clarified the DREAM and took the dreamer through the process and the agony of DELAY to give him time to develop the mission details so he could DECLARE them boldly and clearly.

HOW TO PRIVATELY COMMUNICATE YOUR DIVINE DISTURBANCE

Before we address how Nehemiah went public with his declaration, let's first glean some application principles on how to effectively communicate our Divine Disturbance privately. You've got to learn how to communicate over coffee before you can inspire a crowd.

1. Be Humble

As Nehemiah graciously honored his boss in that moment of conversation, so too must we respect those who have gone before us. The Lord recently had to break me from a hidden habit of disrespect. Some dear friends and mentors of mine lovingly rebuked my pride. Even though I had some big DREAMS—and a divine burden to back it up—it was rubbing people the wrong way, and I didn't even know it. They weren't able to listen to my words because they were so put off by my arrogance. Ouch. The truth hurts. Yet, after repenting and reflecting, I can say that I'm better because of that season of truth.

2. Give the Context

Open the lid on your journey. How did you get here? What were some of the milestones and key events that have shaped you? Invite people into your world. They need to accept *you* before they will accept what you are doing. As John Maxwell regularly says, they will buy into the man (or woman) before they buy into the plan.

3. Lead with the Burden

When you lead with the burden, you allow others to feel the sting of what initially ignited your passion. Your Divine Disturbance is not just a good idea, but a divine imperative. Show them the tension between what currently *is* and what *should be*.

4. Follow with Details

I get so frustrated when I go into meetings led by someone else and there is no clear outline or agenda. We want to know that you've at least thought through this idea enough to consider writing it down. No one likes to have his or her time wasted. When you passionately communicate your Divine Disturbance, you'd better be ready to answer the detail questions that will naturally follow. And when you answer their questions, don't act surprised that these questions are asked. It's a great idea to bounce your Divine Disturbance off a few close friends and allow them to poke holes in it first, before you take it public. This allows you to get your detail ducks in a row.

> **When you passionately communicate your Divine Disturbance, you'd better be ready to answer the detail questions that will naturally follow.**

5. Be Clear

Simplicity is very difficult to achieve. It's easier to be complex. Good communicators take those things that are complicated and make them simple. Make your Divine Disturbance as clear and simple as possible so that people can put their own feet on the pedals and their hands on the handlebars and take the vision to others.

NINE HUNDRED MILES LATER...

Nehemiah began his journey to Jerusalem, armed with ammunition from his earthly king and, most importantly, from his heavenly King. Good thing he had favor, because he was going to need it!

With letters, lumber, and an entire convoy of men accompanying him, Nehemiah made the five-month journey from Susa to Jerusalem. Another five months of waiting and walking. Walking and waiting.

Finally, he arrived in his forefather's hometown. I'm sure upon entering the city of his fathers' tombs, a city he had probably only heard about, a million thoughts rushed through his mind. Nervous, scared, intimidated, he was thinking, "Lord, you got me into this. You're going to have to see this though!"

> So I came to Jerusalem and was there three days. . . . I told no one what my God had put in my heart to do at Jerusalem. (2:11–12)

When I think about Nehemiah first walking into the city of Jerusalem, I remember the movie *Rudy*. Remember when Rudy stands in the Notre Dame tunnel before the only game he's in uniform? He can hear the crowd. He can feel the excitement. And right before he leads the team out onto the field, one of his fellow teammates grabs his face mask and asks him, "Rudy, are you ready for this, champ?" In classic Rudy fashion, he says, "I've been ready for this my whole life!"

So many dreams and good ideas get prematurely aborted because they are communicated to the masses prematurely.

Nehemiah is in the tunnel. He hears all of the reasons flying through his mind why this *can't* be done, and yet, in that moment, he looks heavenward and says, "I've been ready for this my whole life! I was born for this moment! Let's go!"

As he walked onto the field, for three days Nehemiah simply observed the conditions and didn't say a word to anyone why he was there. He held his cards to his chest. He simply observed the devastation of Jerusalem. We're not told what went on through his mind during these three days of inspection. He walked slowly around what was left of the walls. Picked up the rubble with his hands. Examined the gates. Took notes. Imagined what the city must have been like in its glory day. The more rubble he saw, the more his blood started to boil.

After examining the dilapidated walls, I'm sure he started to look in the faces of the citizens of this once-thriving city. Their eyes told it all. Where was the hope? Where was their pride? Where was their passion? It was gone. For 150 years, this was all they had known. Ruin. Rubble. Reproach.

But instead of blurting out what God was up to, he said nothing.

I love what Andy Stanley writes in his amazing book on Nehemiah called *Visioneering*. He says that you are to "Walk before you talk; investigate before you initiate!"[11]

This is the context:

> So I came to Jerusalem and was there three days. Then I arose in the night, I and a few men with me; I told no one what my God had put in my heart to do at Jerusalem; nor was there any animal with me, except

the one on which I rode. And I went out by night through the Valley Gate to the Serpent Well and the Refuse Gate, and viewed the walls of Jerusalem which were broken down and its gates which were burned with fire. Then I went on to the Fountain Gate and to the King's Pool, but there was no room for the animal under me to pass. So I went up in the night by the valley, and viewed the wall; then I turned back and entered by the Valley Gate, and so returned. And the officials did not know where I had gone or what I had done; I had not yet told the Jews, the priests, the nobles, the officials, or the others who did the work. (2:11–16)

Nehemiah walked. And walked. And walked. Even though he had a DREAM bubbling up within him, the king's backing and the divine King's favor, he methodically walked, surveyed, investigated, and prayed.

We can learn a lot from Nehemiah's discipline to remain silent. Most of us impatiently blurt out our "dreams" and "ideas" to anyone who will listen—without fully understanding what we're doing. We blast a message on Twitter or Facebook to the world when we haven't even taken the time to inspect the walls. That's why so many dreams and good ideas get prematurely aborted. It's not that they're bad ideas. It's just that they were communicated to the masses prematurely. And when questions or criticism start to come, the pre-DREAM slips out the door.

MY FIRST ENCOUNTER WITH NEHEMIAH

What I am about to share makes me dewy-eyed every time. It is the reason why this book even exists. It was a defining moment. It was my first encounter with Nehemiah.

I wasn't raised in the church. In fact, the first time I stepped foot into a sanctuary was when I was sixteen years old. There was a pretty girl who wouldn't date me unless I went to church with her. Yeah, you can imagine the rest of the story. I went to church! I explain my whole story in chapter eight, but for now, let's just say that I encountered Jesus in a powerful way. For the first time, I was confronted with my sin and the substitution of Christ as my penalty receiver. I was all-in from that moment.

I'm thankful for a few of my classmates, Ryan Meek and Jesse Robinson among others, who decided to take me under their spiritual wings and help me with what this whole Christianity thing was all about. We had been together on every sports team imaginable growing up and were already close.

But during our sophomore year, after I received salvation, we started to get serious about our faith and reaching our city for Christ. We were just naive enough to believe that God could rock our small town of twenty-five hundred people with the gospel! So we started praying, and planning, and believing.

One night stands out among the rest. After one of our football games, we hung out at Jesse's house playing Nintendo 64 (moment of silence for that playing station). While sitting there, we starting talking about how we could be change agents in our town for Christ. The more we talked, the less we played Nintendo. We started to dream. We started to pray. We started to write down some ideas.

That's when I went over to my new Bible (with the pages still sticking together) and told the guys, "I'm going to take this Bible, close my eyes, and ask God to give us a WORD. This is going to be the Word that guides us to reach our buddies for Christ. This Word is going to give us confidence to move forward with some audacious plans for our town. This is going to be God's Word to us!"

Now, I have to say, I don't recommend this. What if I had thumbed through the pages and landed on Acts 1:18 that says, "Judas had bought a field with the money he received for his treachery. Falling headfirst [hanging himself] there, his body split open, spilling out all his intestines" (NLT). Yeah, not what I had in mind either!

But God was gracious to reward my budding faith, and as I thumbed through the pages of that new Bible, fanning it through my fingers with my eyes locked tight, I landed on Nehemiah 2:17–18. And when I read it, I stood frozen. I couldn't believe it. It was as if the Lord had stopped ruling the universe for one split second in time, looked down to a sixteen-year-old athlete and said, "I want you to have this for your hometown and for the rest of your days!"

Here it is:

> Then I said to them, "You see the distress that we are in, how Jerusalem lies waste, and its gates are burned with fire. Come and let us build the wall of Jerusalem, that we may no longer be a reproach." And I told them of the hand of my God which had been good upon me, and also of the king's words that he had spoken to me.

When I read this verse, in all of my newfound passion, I substituted the word "Jerusalem" with "Spring Hill" and made it my rallying cry for my hometown:

> "You see the distress that we are in, how SPRING HILL lies waste, and its (spiritual) gates are burned with fire. Come and let us build the wall of SPRING HILL, that we may no longer be a reproach."

Holy cow.

Ryan, Jesse, and I stopped right there, got on our knees and thanked God for what he had just shown us. That verse became our true north. Over the next couple of years, we saw over one hundred of our classmates, teachers, and staff in our high school give their lives to Christ! Mind you, we had *less than four hundred people* in our entire school. God let me see a glimpse of an explosive revival, and sometimes when I close my eyes, I still remember the brightness of the fireworks.

I've been consumed with these two verses ever since that day. I'm fascinated with them. These two verses might just be the tipping point that takes your Divine Disturbance from where it is to where God wants it to be.

THE STAGE IS SET

After Nehemiah's three-day investigation tour, he finally gathered everyone in the city. I'm sure the citizens were wondering what these foreigners were doing in their hometown. Butterflies had formed again in the bartender's belly. It was one thing to communicate your DREAM to one or two people over coffee, but how should he paint the picture to a larger audience? With everyone's eyes on him, Nehemiah started by stating the obvious. He began with the problem.

1. The Problem (Brutal Facts)

> "You see the distress that we are in, how Jerusalem lies waste and its gates have been burned with fire." (17)

He had them look around and view their city from a different perspective. They might not have viewed their situation as distressed. But they were. Also notice that Nehemiah said, "we." He didn't come in and say, "YOU people are in distress and I'M the only one able to clean up YOUR mess!" No. He placed himself in their shoes and said, "We are in distress."

As he outlined the problem—the city "lies waste and its gates have been burned with fire"—I'm sure that the people's natural response would have been, "Yep. Tell us something we don't know!" But they had grown accustomed to the rubble. They passed it every-day on their way to do business or go to school. They had never seen a flourishing Jerusalem, just a dilapidated one.

Isn't it the same in our lives? When I speak, I love to ask the audience this question, "How many of you have a crack in your windshield?" Usually about 20 percent of the people raise their hands. Then I ask, "How many of you have had a crack in your windshield for longer than you initially intended?" All the wind-shield-crack owners keep their hands raised. They haven't gotten it fixed because they have grown accustomed to it. It has become familiar to them. In fact, some could be driving around in a car with a spider web of cracked glass filling the entire windshield, and simply see right through it.

Why? Because that which is familiar *in* our lives loses its effect *on* our lives.

The rubble was familiar. They looked right past it. They didn't see anything wrong with it. And because it was familiar, it lost its effect.

So, when Nehemiah spoke, his words jolted them out of their comfortable coma. He was the one who had the courage to say, "Things aren't good! We're in trouble here! Wake up, people!" This was their 9/11 moment. This was when everything changed. Finally, they saw the brutal reality of the situation. And when they heard his words, they were embarrassed that they had let the situation get that bad without doing anything about it.

Remember back to chapter one? Nehemiah allowed the brutal facts of reality to sink into his soul and bring about a Divine Disturbance. Now, he simply communicated that same Divine Disturbance to the people who would help see his DREAM become a reality. He led with the problem. And so should we.

> **As we communicate our Divine Disturbance to people, we must lead with what *is*, before we cast the vision for what *could be*.**

As we communicate our Divine Disturbance to people, we must lead with what *is*, before we cast the vision for what *could be*. We need to spread like wildfire the unacceptability of "where we are now" and spark a burning desire for change.

If you have a Divine Disturbance for your marriage, you might need to lead with "Honey, I believe that where we are is not where God wants us to be. We lack communication. We lack intimacy. We're living on different pages in completely opposite books. Let's be honest, we're merely roommates here."

If your Divine Disturbance is for your church, you might lead with "Who are we kidding, here? We haven't seen a baptism in twelve months. The only people who come to our church are those who feel obligated to attend. Our building and ministries are antiquated. Something's got to change!"

In communicating the problem, it's not that we need people to learn something new. It's usually that they need to be reminded of what they already know.

2. The Solution

> "Come and let us build the wall of Jerusalem, that we may no longer be a reproach." (17)

Everyone was aware that something needed to be done. It just took someone with enough courage to actually say it. Andy Stanley says, "Whereas a clear explanation of the problem engages the mind, the solution engages the imagination."[12] People need to have freedom to dream.

Walt Disney was a dreamer who could paint mental pictures better than almost anyone. The story is told that, at his funeral, some said they were sad he would never see Epcot come into fruition. (It hadn't yet been built.) Someone who was close to Disney responded, "No, if Walt dreamed it—he saw it more fully realized than anyone else ever will!"

You might need permission to let your mind drift a bit regarding your dreams. It's okay, really. Go ahead. Imagine. Wonder. Daydream. Paint the picture with clarity and detail. What does it look like? What does it feel like? What does it smell like?

"WHAT IF" AND "IMAGINE"

Three of the most powerful words in the English language are "What if..." and "Imagine..."

What if your dream really were realized?

What if your business really did make enough money to fund an entire missions endeavor?

What if your family really did become missionaries in India?

What if you were to write that book? And what if that book became a New York Times best seller?

Imagine the stories you could tell your grandkids.

Imagine how you could change the circumstances of an entire people group.

Imagine how many people you'd find enjoying heaven because you made a difference in what they believed.

Imagine kneeling before Jesus and hearing, "Well done."

What if.

Imagine.

That's what Nehemiah did for the people of Jerusalem. He painted the picture of "what if" and "imagine." That's what you need to do as well. Start with the problem, but state your Divine Disturbance as the solution to the problem in terms that help people find themselves in God's larger story.

3. The Why

He also told the citizens *why* they needed to rebuild. Did you catch that? I hope you're starting to notice a theme here too. *Why* is everywhere in this narrative. It's extremely important. As Michael Hyatt often says, "When you lose your *why*, you'll lose your *way*." Nehemiah explains, "Come and let us build the wall of Jerusalem, *that we may no longer be a reproach*."

For him, these were not merely walls. They were the character and reputation of God himself. Broken-down and burned walls meant that God's people were missing their full potential and that God's name was receiving contempt rather than glory! God's people had become the laughing stock of the world. If it were an NFL game, the fans would have put paper grocery bags on their heads in shame. And that shame was offensive to Nehemiah.

4. The When

He not only said that they needed to rebuild, they needed to rebuild *now*. They didn't have a moment to spare. Now, hold the phone. If I were sitting there listening to this speech by Nehemiah, my heart probably would have been moved too. I'm sure he was convincing and passionate. But the walls had been in this condition for 150 years. Why, I probably would have thought, should I start to rebuild *now*?

Nehemiah pointed to current activity—how God had orchestrated all of these events. He said, "And I told them of the hand of my God which had been good upon me, and also the king's words that he had spoken to me" (2:18). I'm not sure what all he explained to them, but I am sure he had rehearsed it several times. I'm sure he started from the day his world changed, when his brother, Hanani, came to him while he was still in Susa. I'm sure that he talked about how, for four long months,

> **He told them the story. He invited them into the process.**

he fasted, prayed, wept, prayed, and planned for this moment. I'm sure that he told them how he was "dreadfully afraid" when the king asked him what was the matter, but then, to his surprise, the king showed favor and grace not only to let him come rebuild the city, but also to have letters, lumber, and a convoy. I'm sure the he shared with them the fact that for three days he walked around the city's walls and kept everything silent—for the sake of this moment.

He told them the story. He invited them into the process. He shared with them how God was miraculously weaving his master plan into existence and that he, the creator of the universe, wanted *them* to be his partners in seeing this DREAM become reality.

After he shared these stories that he had rehearsed for the past nine months, once he finished his last sentence, I'm sure that there was an awkward pause. Although this pause probably lasted only a few milliseconds, it felt like an eternity. For in this pause, after you communicate your Divine Disturbance and before the people respond, the weight is enormous. The pressure is legit. And every dreamer knows this moment is a scary place to inhabit. It's the moment on the high dive when you've just crossed the point of no return. No going back now. Now or never.

And to Nehemiah's amazement, this is what happened:

> So they said, "Let us rise up and build." Then they set their hands to do this good work. (18)

This was a great moment in biblical history. As I place myself in the story, I can hear the cheers and feel the excitement. I can see the high fives and the fist bumps. Heads nod. People smile. Life is good. At least for now.

I HAVE A DREAM

When considering how to cast a compelling vision for a preferred future as Nehemiah did, we need look no further than Dr. Martin Luther King's resonant "I Have a Dream" address. You may not realize that, as Dr. King stood on the Washington Mall addressing, for all intents, the nation, the "I Have a Dream" portion—the portion that everyone knows, that everyone remembers, that captured the world's attention—those eloquent words came eleven minutes into the speech!

I've watched the recordings of this speech dozens of times, and every time I'm spellbound by what takes place. In the first eleven minutes, you can tell Dr. King is reading his notes and wanting to make sure that he stays on script. Who would want to tank a speech in front of two million people? He speaks of a promissory note that the disenfranchised African Americans were going to cash. It was a good metaphor.

Yet, eleven minutes into his talk, he realized that this new speech wasn't connecting in the way that he wanted. He was losing his audience. And if you're a communicator, and you lose two million people, you might as well pack it in! So he did what any good speaker would do—he trashed his speech. He reverted back to the words, the phrases, the images, and the cadence that he had used in churches and meeting halls in the previous three years.

> **So he did what any good speaker would do—he trashed his speech.**

And what were those words, images, and stories?

> I have a dream that one day on the red hills of Georgia the sons of former slaves and the sons of former slave owners will be able to sit down together at the table of brotherhood...I have a dream that my four little children will one day live in a nation where they will not be judged by the color of their skin, but by the content of their character. I have a dream today![13]

Why did he revert back to his old speeches? Because they were the essence of his Divine Disturbance! Those images, pictures, stories, and feelings had moved thousands of people in smaller settings, and he knew they would work in front of millions. Even when people close to Dr. King tried to get him to use different word pictures and images, he reverted back to what came from inside his own soul—*his* words that came from his divine burden. When Dr. King said, "I have a dream," it's because he had a DREAM.

Nehemiah communicated the essence of his Divine Disturbance in words that came from his soul. That is what you must do as well. State the problem and then paint the picture of the future with clarity. Why should we listen? How has God brought this about? What can I do to join you?

Bringing your Divine Disturbance out in public is a scary thing. You will have butterflies. You will be tempted to remain silent. The frog will be lodged in your throat. But you *must* speak.

When you do, an amazing thing will happen. Other dreamers will catch your vision and feel your Divine Disturbance. It will become contagious. Watch out—a movement is about to ensue.

MAKING IT REAL

- If we went to coffee, would you be able to articulate to me your Divine Disturbance with only a napkin? If no, practice. If yes, what is it?

- What is the problem your Divine Disturbance solves?

- What is your "why"?

- What is your "what"? Write down the details of your plan.

- Since pictures and stories empower communication, what are some images and examples that you can use to help make your Divine Disturbance stick?

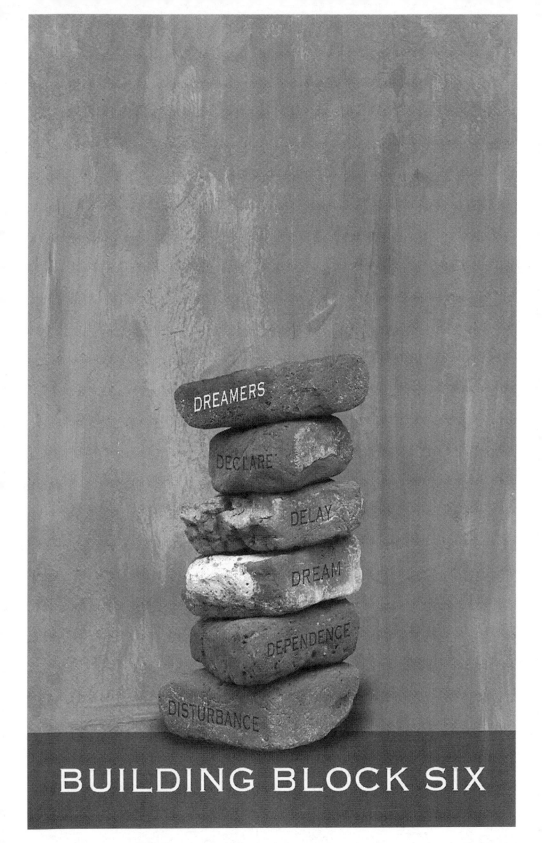

BUILDING BLOCK SIX

Building Block 6:

DREAMERS

"Shut up, shut up, I am busy. I am working!"
—Senior wireless operator, the Titanic

The great boxer Muhammad Ali terrorized his opponents both in and out of the ring. He was the world's greatest, and he let everyone know it! He would mesmerize press conferences with bold declarations of his awesomeness.

One time, as he sat in first class on an airplane, a stewardess politely approached him and said, "Mr. Ali, you're going to need to put on your seatbelt."

The other passengers froze. *Oh no she didn't!*

"You don't know who I am, do you? I'm Superman! I'm the greatest! Superman don't need to put on no seatbelt!"

Without skipping a beat, this stewardess snapped back and said, "Last time I checked, Superman didn't need an airplane! Now put your belt on!"

Newsflash. You're not Superman.

And you need help.

Whatever wall you're trying to build, whatever Divine Disturbance is rattling in your brain, you're going to need help—lots of help. No God-sized dream can be accomplished alone. Think how foolish it would have been for Nehemiah to try to accomplish this rebuilding work all by himself.

Besides, people are sundials waiting in the shade. They are waiting for permission. They are begging for someone to come along and pull the best out of them, to invite them to a better life and a bigger cause. They are waiting to piggyback on your dream. Don't rob them of an opportunity to help. And when your Divine Disturbance intersects with what God's been doing in someone's life, that's where you'll find a great partnership.

People are sundials waiting in the shade. They are waiting for permission. They are begging for someone to come along and pull the best out of them.

Nehemiah was not the first person who wanted to rebuild Jerusalem's walls. I'm sure that every other year some hotshot with a "dream" wanted to rebuild. But Nehemiah was different. He leveraged other DREAMERS to join the cause.

Initially, in this book's infancy as a simple, thirty-minute sermon, I almost overlooked Nehemiah 3. Why? It's just a bunch of names and duties of hundreds of people who were building the wall. Depending on your Bible translation, the word "next" (as in "next to him") occurs over twenty-five times in this one chapter. Look at these five verses alone:

> **Next** to him, the repairs were made by the Levites
> under Rehum son of Bani. **Beside** him, Hashabiah,
> ruler of half the district of Keilah, carried out repairs
> for his district. **Next** to him, the repairs were made
> by their fellow Levites under Binnui son of Henadad,

ruler of the other half-district of Keilah. **Next** to him, Ezer son of Jeshua, ruler of Mizpah, repaired another section, from a point facing the ascent to the armory as far as the angle of the wall. **Next** to him, Baruch son of Zabbai zealously repaired another section, from the angle to the entrance of the house of Eliashib the high priest. **Next** to him, Meremoth son of Uriah, the son of Hakkoz, repaired another section, from the entrance of Eliashib's house to the end of it. (3:17–21; NIV)

If God is going to do something magnificent in and through you, you need people "next to" you—shoulder to shoulder. According to the size of your Divine Disturbance is your need for shoulders next door. You might need a handful or an army. The key questions you should ask are:

Who needs to be next to me?
> (Who do you need to *recruit*?)

Whom do I need to be next to?
> (With whom do you need to *partner*?
> Who should you help?)

Although we "know" that partnership and teamwork are important, there's still a part of us that wants to do everything ourselves. We have this little voice of pride that wells up in our ears and says, "You don't need help. You can do it on your own. You don't need advice."

That's fine. If you want to sink like the *Titanic*, go ahead and ignore this chapter.

SHUT UP, SHUT UP, I AM BUSY. I AM WORKING!

It's been over one hundred years, yet the images of devastation still haunt us.

The date:	April 15, 1912.
The location:	The Atlantic Ocean between New York Harbor and Liverpool, England.
The event:	The maiden voyage of the *Titanic*.

This enormously elaborate vessel was touted as "the unsinkable" ship. It was meticulously made and was the "Pride of the White Star Line." In 1912 a ticket on the maiden voyage of the famed *Titanic* was priceless. Celebrities from all over the world clamored for a chance to make this trip.

Dripping with arrogance, the crewmembers and captain laughingly said, "God himself can't sink this ship!" Yet, on her way from England to New York, gliding through a calm sea, the crew of the *Titanic* started receiving several warnings of icebergs floating off the coast of Newfoundland. Many of the other ships in that area of the Atlantic Ocean had stopped travel for the night because of the warnings.

Dripping with arrogance, the crewmembers and captain laughingly said, "God himself can't sink this ship!"

In fact, reports say that even other *ships* issued stern warnings to the *Titanic* about the impending icebergs. These warnings were "violently rebuked" by Jack Phillips, the *Titanic's* senior wireless operator. Phillips, who seemed to be greatly annoyed at this interruption from other ships, is tragically quoted as keying this message back to those who were trying to warn him: "Shut up, shut up, I am busy. I am working!"[14]

Yes, you read that right. "Shut up, shut up, I am busy. I am working!"

Although the crew saw the icebergs, they could not wrap their minds around the sheer magnitude of possible destruction. They were looking at the surface and never took into account what lurked underneath.

Even though they tried to turn away at the last second to avoid the collision, it was too late. The underbelly of the massive vessel scraped the side of an iceberg, which penetrated its shell and caused it to fill with ice-cold, Atlantic Ocean water.

Two hours and forty minutes later, the "unsinkable ship"— the ship that "God himself couldn't sink"—upended and sank, carrying 1,503 innocent men, women, and children to their premature deaths. Only 705 passengers and crew survived as they hoarded space in half-filled lifeboats.

This is the tragic story of a disaster that could have been prevented if one man had swallowed his pride and listened to the advice of others. If he had allowed others to help, 1,503 people might have lived.

Wouldn't it be a tragedy if this process—God breaking your heart for what breaks his, giving you a DREAM for what could and should be—if this process came to a screeching halt because you were too insecure to ask for help?

It takes a great deal of humility to ask for help. Because in asking for help, you admit that there's something you *can't* do—you can't do this thing alone.

> **It takes a great deal of humility to ask for help. Because in asking for help, you admit that there's something you *can't* do—you can't do this thing alone.**

WHO ARE THE PEOPLE NEXT TO YOU?

Let me give you some of my examples for how this looks. I pray
that you'll be able to find yourself in my story and connect the dots
to your own Divine Disturbance.

Although I'm a pastor, and I study the Bible as my job, my
marriage wasn't where it needed to be. I was giving marital advice
to others; I *wasn't* getting marital advice for my own marriage. So
I took a humble pill and made the most important call I've ever
made—to a Christian counselor. Fran and I had a DREAM for our
marriage—to build a wall of legacy and faithfulness. But we couldn't
do it alone. We needed someone to come "next to" us and give us
insight, encouragement, and support that we couldn't have gotten
otherwise.

If God has broken you over the condition of your marriage, you
are going to need to recruit others to help. You might need to confess
that you don't have it all figured out and you need a counselor.

You might have to get creative in how you get others to come
next to you and help your DREAM. Recently, the Lord DISTURBED
me over my financial condition. We were in debt and lazy with
our money. At the end of the month, we would look and say, "We
spend *that* much money on eating out! Seriously!" We weren't saving
and giving as much as we should have been. Honestly, we had let
the busyness of life take control of our finances. Something had to
change.

So I went to the local library and checked out every book and
audio book that I could get my hands on regarding budgeting,
spending, saving, giving, and so on. We took Dave Ramsey's
Financial Peace University course. Again. We're not there yet, but
because of the people "next to" us—these authors and financial

wizards—we've started to climb out of the mess we were in. In fact, God has given me a DREAM to become a reverse tither. That means that I would give 90 percent of my income away and live on the remaining 10. In order to do that, I'm going to need some help!

Maybe you have a large decision that's in front of you and you're not sure what to do. You're going to need advice. When I was in college, I had to make a huge decision. I went to school on a full-ride baseball scholarship, but a few months into it, the Lord DISTURBED me over the spiritual condition of my generation. I felt the promptings to hang up my spikes and go into the ministry. Whatever my decision, I knew I would let someone down.

So what did I do? I recruited a makeshift "Board of Advisors" to help me navigate this decision. I called six people of various ages and backgrounds whom I respected and asked for two meetings with them. I explained the situation and my dilemma. They all weighed in and gave their advice. Then it was up to me to make the final decision. I am forever grateful for those advisors.

ASSEMBLING YOUR PIT CREW

What about you? Who are the people you need to recruit? Who are the people that you need to join? In his book *Get Off Your "But,"* Sean Stephenson talks about a pit crew and a racecar driver. Although one person sits behind the wheel, it takes a village of people to support and bring the whole team to a victory. Each person knows his or her role. When everyone works together, they all have a greater chance of winning.

As you are building your team, remember that *teams* are well-rounded—people are not. Let me say that again. *Teams* are well-rounded,

Teams are well-rounded, people are not.

people are not. Your goal for building your team should be to find people who complement your strengths, weaknesses, passions, and abilities. You don't need everyone to be the same as you—otherwise at least one of you is unneeded!

Additionally, just because a certain job or task might seem awful to you, it might be the job that makes someone else come alive. You might rather stick a fork in your eye than work all day on an Excel spreadsheet. Working on that same Excel spreadsheet for eight hours a day might bring someone else incredible amounts of joy. Avoid making other people's decisions for them. Avoid assuming that a job is either above them or below them. How do you know what the Lord is doing in their hearts at this exact moment? Maybe they are asking God to allow them to use their gifts for the very thing that your Divine Disturbance is striving to solve.

In thinking about the various roles that people play in the pit crew, I'm reminded about a John F. Kennedy story. While visiting the NASA headquarters, JFK once stopped to talk with a man who was holding a mop.

"And what do you do?" President Kennedy asked.

The man, a janitor, replied, "I'm helping to put a man on the moon, sir."

JFK had painted the vision clear enough to the American people so that everyone viewed his or her own job as essential to completing the task of getting a man on the moon. Now that's what I'm talking about—bringing a team together for a larger purpose!

BUT WHAT IF PEOPLE DON'T HELP?

Let me break it to you. There will be many who simply will *not* jump on board with your Divine Disturbance. They might be vocal about it, or they might quietly refuse to cooperate. That's normal. I'd say that if you got *everyone* immediately involved, I'd have to look for the red juice you were serving in your fortified compound.

Nehemiah faced this rebuff from a group of "nobles." It says in Nehemiah 3:5 that "the Tekoites made repairs; but their nobles did not put their shoulders to the work of the their Lord." We're not told exactly why the Tekoite nobles didn't work. Maybe they were lazy. Maybe they didn't like construction. Maybe they were injured. But more than likely, they didn't like to be told what to do, and they surely didn't like this young hotshot coming into the *their* city telling them what to do and how to do it. It didn't matter what Nehemiah would have done to try to persuade these nobles, they weren't going to do squat.

> I'd say that if you got *everyone* immediately involved, I'd have to look for the red juice you were serving in your fortified compound.

NOOSE 101

I can relate. For some strange reason, I've always found myself in water way over my head when it comes to leadership. I'm constantly the youngest person around the table. God must have a sense of humor that way.

One church leadership meeting stands out above the rest. I was a nineteen-year-old senior pastor who had a vision to change the world. Yes, I was probably a hothead. Okay, I *was* a hothead. But my desire was sincere at least. I had been a Christian for a mere two and a half years before accepting the role as Senior Pastor of itty-bitty Sandy Level Baptist Church in Goodview, Virginia. We had fifty people on a good day.

Well, I made some minor judgment errors. First I painted the church without consulting the building committee. Then I changed the sign out front without garnering a vote. Next, we started using transparencies in our worship services. God forbid. (Remember transparencies? High-tech stuff.)

Well, one guy in our church had enough of this blasted change. He was going to run me out. I remember one morning at six thirty as I got ready for school in the church parsonage, this guy showed up at my house, walked right in because he had a key (oh, God bless the church parsonage), got up in my face and said he wanted to kill me! That's right, kill me!

That night we had an emergency leadership team meeting to discuss this. Sure enough, this man came barging into our meeting carrying a noose! He took the noose, slammed it on the conference room table, and said, "There's gonna be a hangin' in here tonight and it's gonna be the preacher!"

Needless to say, this man was like the Tekoite nobles. Regardless of what I did or didn't do, this man just wasn't going to like me. I wonder if the Tekoite nobles ever went to Nehemiah with a noose. Wouldn't surprise me.

Here's the point. You need to run with those who are running and avoid fretting over the people who've left the stadium. You can either fritter away your DREAM complaining about the few that boycott, or you can be grateful for the several with feet already on the ground, racing to find stones for your wall.

DUCK HUNTING

To communicate this same point, my mentor, Dr. Tim Elmore, uses the analogy of duck hunting. Some of you might think I deserved lynching in the story above—perhaps, for you, this illustration will put the cat—or, in this case, the duck—in the bag. Imagine a man who goes out early in the morning duck hunting and comes back with thirty ducks. When his wife asks him how the hunt went, can you imagine him saying something like, "I had a horrible time! I let fifty get away!" No. He wouldn't say that. He would focus on the thirty that he brought home. It's the same way with building our teams for accomplishing our Divine Disturbance. Avoid focusing on the ones that got away. Be grateful for the ones who are with you, and move forward.

MAKING IT REAL:

- "Who needs to be next to me?" (Who do you need to recruit?)

- What roles need to be filled in order to move my Divine Disturbance forward?

- Who are the people who have assisted me in my journey thus far that I need to thank personally?

- "Whom do I need to be next to?" (With whom do you need to partner? Who should you help?)

BUILDING BLOCK SEVEN

Building Block 7:

DEMONS

"There's no reason to fire cannons at sparrows."
—*Jerry Falwell*

Light attracts bugs. Bank on it.

It's not a matter of *if* you will be attacked, but when. How you will respond?

We war for the souls of men. We're storming across the battle-field not strolling through the park. Since all Divine Disturbances are forged in the flames of what's wrong in the world (or in your world), they will naturally come under attack. Our DREAMS invade enemy territory.

The apostle Paul, in Ephesians 6:11–12, commands us to "Put on the whole armor of God, that you may be able to stand against the wiles of the devil. For we do not wrestle against flesh and blood, but against principalities, against powers, against the rulers of the darkness of this age, against spiritual hosts of wickedness in the heavenly places."

161

Translation: If it bleeds, it's not your enemy!

If you think that a person is your enemy—or a group of people are your enemies—think again. They might play the enemy role to sidetrack you from your main mission— but they are merely pawns in the larger chess game.

Consider:

> Your ex-spouse.
> Your boss.
> Your neighbor.
> Your current spouse.
> Your mother-in-law.
> Your co-worker.
> Your parents.
> That group of people.
> Your old church.

When you realize that none of these people or groups is your enemy, the knowledge is both freeing and scary. People remain sundials in the shade because they know that once they reveal that dream, it will be criticized, attacked, and mocked. Once they reveal their dream, they will discover their DEMONS. Especially if the dream centers on helping others and reaching people with the gospel.

In Nehemiah's case, a handful of local government leaders despised his taking an interest in Jerusalem. Why? Because his interest threatened them. So, they unleashed an all-out assault of lies, criticism, mockery, and confusion in an attempt to stop God's work from being accomplished.

If it bleeds, it's not your enemy!

If you want a test case for how attacks work, go no further than the middle chapters of Nehemiah.

We see first that the enemy attacks on three fronts— internally, externally, and spiritually.

Internal Attacks

These are the voices in our heads that tell us we can't do it. We don't have what it takes. They are the DEMONS of doubt. (We'll cover these more in the next chapter.)

External Attacks

These are people or circumstances that put on the brakes, expecting your dream to come to a grinding halt. They are the DEMONS of obstruction.

Spiritual Attacks

There are times when both internal and external attacks fail, and the devil makes an all-out blitz on your life. If you are a Christian, the devil can't possess you because the Holy Spirit and Satan can't have dual residence. But our great enemy will try to thwart your progress by oppressing and depressing you to the point of inaction and failure. These are the DEMONS of the air. At full power.

Sound fun? Why in the world would any of us walk willingly into attacks like these?

"No, man, I'm good," you say. "This Susa sundial is perfectly content in the shade."

One of my favorite quotes regarding criticism came from former President Theodore Roosevelt. He eloquently put the critic in his rightful place. He said:

It's not the critic who counts. It's not the man who points out how the strong man stumbled. Credit belongs to the man who really was in the arena, his face marred by dust, sweat, and blood, who strives valiantly, who errs to come short and short again, because there is no effort without error and shortcoming. It is the man who actually strives to do the deeds, who knows the great enthusiasm and knows the great devotion, who spends himself on a worthy cause, who at best, knows in the end the triumph of great achievement. And, who at worst, if he fails, at least fails while daring greatly, so that his place shall never be with those cold and cruel souls who know neither victory nor defeat.[15]

All DREAMERS will face DEMONS. But, then, *so will sundials.* You can either be the cold soul who knows "neither victory nor defeat." Or you can dare greatly. The choice is yours to make.

SIX WAYS THE ENEMY TRIES TO DERAIL YOU

Remember, light attracts bugs. And the devil is a blood-sucking mosquito. You won't be able to prevent every mosquito from sticking its vampire beak in you, but you might be able to slap many of them dead before they inject their venom under your skin.

1. Your Enemy Will Use Accusations

What happens to you when someone falsely accuses you of something? If you're like me, your blood starts to boil and your mind races to defend yourself.

What will you do if someone accuses you of having ill motives?

"They're only doing that to get promoted!"

"They're only doing that so that they can be seen!"

"He's really stealing from the company...don't you know that?"

Immediately after the magnificent 2:17–18 moment, when Nehemiah rallied the troops with his "I Have a Dream" speech, the very next verse says this:

> But when Sanballat the Horonite, Tobiah the Ammonite official, and Geshem the Arab heard of it, they laughed at us and despised us, and said, "What is this thing that you are doing? Will you rebel against the king?" (19)

These cronies accused Nehemiah of rebelling against the king! Seriously? They had used this tactic previously and it worked. Remember, Nehemiah's efforts to rebuild were the third rebuilding wave. The first wave came a few years prior to rebuild the temple. When they started building, look at what these same enemies did:

> Then the people of the land tried to discourage the people of Judah. They troubled them in building, and hired counselors against them to frustrate their purpose. . . . They wrote an accusation against the inhabitants of Judah and Jerusalem. (Ezra 4:4–6)

And the result of this written accusation to stop the temple? The construction ceased. The plan of God momentarily stopped. The enemy won.

But not this time!

Check out Nehemiah's immediate response:

> So I answered them, and said to them, "The God
> of heaven Himself will prosper us; therefore we His
> servants will arise and build, but you have no heritage
> or right or memorial in Jerusalem." (Nehemiah 2:20)

I love how focused Nehemiah was. He didn't let their accusations steer him in the least. Why? Because he wasn't a people pleaser. He was God pleaser.

When people falsely accuse you of something, do you spend your time and energy trying to prove your innocence, or do you acknowledge their accusation and then move on to building your wall? I remember with vivid clarity the day I had to choose whether to respond to false accusations as Ezra's temple builders had or as Nehemiah had.

When people falsely accuse you of something, do you spend your time and energy trying to prove your innocence, or do you acknowledge their accusation and then move on to building your wall?

Firing Cannons At Sparrows

The principle became clear to me when I worked in 2004 as the assistant to the late Dr. Jerry Falwell (he founded Liberty University and pastored a twenty-four-thousand-member church in Virginia). Here I was, a twenty-two-year-old kid, full of passion, and whose life motto was "Ready, FIRE, Aim." One of my assignments was to do research for TV interviews. About once a week, one of the national news outlets would request an interview.

I'll never forget one time when one of the big boys—ABC, NBC, CBS (I'm not going to tell you which one)—came out and interviewed for four hours. I was right there the whole time, saw the entire thing. Then, sitting on my couch the next day watching the evening news, I was shocked at how they had edited out almost everything Dr. Falwell had said and spun it according to what they wanted. I was furious.

The next day, I stormed into the office ready to take down that TV network single-handedly if I needed to. I barged into Dr. Falwell's office expecting him to be furious too. I said, "Did you watch the interview last night?"

"Yes."

"And...???"

"And it was good."

"What? It was terrible! They took everything out of context and spun your words to match their agenda! How can that be good?"

He then told me, in his booming voice, "Young Phillip, I've been doing this for fifty years. I've made a lot of mistakes, and I've learned a lot through the years. I'm never surprised when lost people act lost. I know you're upset. I was too when I was your age. But I've learned through my failures that there's no reason to fire cannons at sparrows! God's a big God. He knows our hearts, and that's all that matters."

Talk about perspective.

There's no reason to fire cannons at sparrows!

> I'm never surprised when lost people act lost. . . . God's a big God. He knows our hearts, and that's all that matters.
> —Jerry Falwell

That kind of advice has carried me while in the ministry. Believe it or not, many, many people in the "church-world" despise change. Change, in their minds, is the cardinal sin. "We've never done it that way before," they sing. Their mission statement: "Preacher, we own you." Remember the noose? At times, I have needed trusted people to follow me home from leadership meetings because I feared for my life. Updating the church's color and the bulletin really hacks some people off!

Seriously! I can't make this stuff up. Even when the majority membership of a church has agreed to a change, some folks still dream of lynching the pastor.

In thinking about accusations, I'm reminded of this quote by Marcus Tullius Cicero: "As fire when thrown into water is cooled down and put out, so also a false accusation when brought against a man of the purest and holiest character, boils over and is at once dissipated...himself standing unmoved."

So, if you are facing unfair accusations, take heart. You are in great company. God knows your heart. God knows your motives. You should sleep well at night.

2. Your Enemy Will Use Questions

This tactic has been around since the Garden of Eden when Satan questioned God's Word by saying, "Did God *really* say, 'You must not eat from any tree in the garden'?" (Genesis 3:1; NIV; emphasis mine).

I am a huge proponent of questions. I love asking the right kind of questions to the right people at the right time. I had to learn this the hard way.

The best leader is the best question asker. They ask the right questions at the right time to the right people.

At first, I thought I had to have all of the answers and be a "Leader" with a capital *L* on my chest. Well, that didn't work. I wasn't fooling anyone. So I had to change my game.

I discovered that the best leader doesn't have to have all of the answers. The best leader is the best question asker. They ask the right questions at the right time to the right people. Then they leverage the influence of those with more experience and knowledge to push the ball down the field.

Questions are powerful.

Questions are painful, if used negatively.

That's what we see happening in Nehemiah 4. The workers are building the wall with joy. They have sacrificed so much to partner with God to make this happen. But then they start getting peppered with questions from their enemies. These questions are focused and painful. They are meant to thwart the plan of God in the city.

> But it so happened, when Sanballat heard that we were rebuilding the wall, that he was furious and very indignant, and mocked the Jews. And he spoke before his brethren and the army of Samaria, and said, "What are these feeble Jews doing? Will they fortify themselves? Will they offer sacrifices? Will they complete it in a day? Will they revive the stones from the heaps of rubbish—stones that are burned?" (1–2)

Did you count them? Five. Five questions in rapid-fire sequence. See if these questions hit home with you:

a. "What are these feeble Jews doing?"

This question was laden with sarcasm. It was almost as if the bigger, more popular bully was standing across the playground, mocking them with a baby voice: "Oh, look at little Billy. Is he going to play football today with the Big Boys?"

You might have heard similar questions like:

- Who do you think you are?

- Do you *really* think you're a good enough leader to do this?

- Do you *really* think that people will follow you?

- Do you think that someone of your race and nationality can *actually* accomplish that?

b. "Will they fortify themselves?"

This question tried to make the builders doubt their ability to accomplish the task. It inferred that they needed extra help fortifying their city—that they couldn't do it themselves. Well, in part, their criticism was absolutely right. They *couldn't* do it by themselves. That's where their DEPENDENT prayer kicked in. They weren't doing it. God was.

Do the following words sound familiar?

- You've never finished anything, what makes you think that you'll follow through with this project?

- You realize that no one in your family *ever* has done something like this, right?

c. "Will they offer sacrifices?"

This question, though it may look innocent, dripped with evil. Sanballat questioned their relationship with God. Mind you, he was probably the mastermind behind stopping the temple work too. He didn't want them making sacrifices because he probably knew that once they got right with God, his game was over.

And if you are doing something noteworthy for the Kingdom, you'd better believe that people are going to question your sincerity—even your Christianity.

These sound familiar?

- I though you were a Christian. And you operate your business like *that*?

- Oh, now that you're all "holier than thou," you probably don't want to associate with people like *me*, do you?

- You think that just because you go to church, you're better than us, don't you?

d. "Will they complete it in a day?"

This was a question of performance and pace. Sanballat questioned if they even knew what they were attempting to do. He knew that the workers were working at a record-setting pace. They were passionate. They all "had a mind to work," and it looked like nothing would get in their way.

If Sanballat were here today, he would probably say something to you like:

- Seriously, don't you think you've taken this Christianity thing a bit too far?

- Slow down. Do you think that you can *really* change the world this fast?

- You realize that you're just one person, right?

> *e. "Will they revive the stones from the heaps*
> *of rubbish—stones that are burned?"*

These stones had been scattered on the ground, untouched for 150 years—not to mention they were also burned and, therefore, weakened bricks. The "heaps of rubbish" referred to the massive amount of work in front of them. Sanballat wanted them to believe the task was too great. The mountain too tall. The journey too long.

Maybe you've heard questions like:

- This is just the way things are around here. Don't you realize that?

- Wake up, son. This is the way we do it in *this* church. Didn't anyone tell you?

- You're trying to tackle a huge problem. You're just one person. What difference can you *really* make?

3. Your Enemy Will Use Humiliation

"Sticks and stones may break my bones but words can never hurt me." Yeah right. As if accusations and a barrage of questions weren't enough, the builders heard this from their enemy.

> Now Tobiah the Ammonite was beside him, and he said, "Whatever they build, if even a fox goes up on it, he will break down their stone wall." (4:3)

That was the Old Testament equivalent of a "Yo mamma's so ugly..." joke. Foxes are some of the most light-footed creatures. They can swiftly and discreetly walk across tree limbs. Saying that if even a fox goes up on the wall, it will break down was a slap in the face. Tobiah was shouting off some pretty heavy doses of attempted humiliation, aimed directly at the builder's competence.

That was the Old Testament equivalent of a "Yo mamma's so ugly..." joke.

Words meant to humiliate can hit you in the gut. But if we can remember the famous words of Mother Teresa, "We learn humility through accepting humiliations cheerfully," I think we'll be okay. Don't take yourself too seriously. If people try to make fun of you, let them.

People constantly make fun of me. I just smile, nod, and pray that lightning strikes them down.

Just kidding.

Sometimes.

Our enemy, Satan, likes to make humiliation his tool when a project or relationship fails. Notice that I said "project" and "relationship." When something that we have done fails to succeed as well as we had hoped, Satan uses that moment to call *us* a failure. And with failure, naturally, comes humiliation—*if* our identity is wrapped up in our project or relationship.

One of the key core values of Grace Church, where I have served on staff, is Allowing Risks. Now, let's avoid misunderstandings here—we weren't *risky* in how we operated. But we strived to cultivate a culture of allowing risks. How could we do this? We recognized that our identity was not measured in the project, but rather in Christ.

Do you know how freeing this is? We tried some pretty dumb experiments in the past several years that totally flopped. We measured that a success. Because if we tried ten new ways of doing something and nine of them flopped, one of them was destined to be great!

The only way that you can be humiliated is if you allow the other people's vain comments to shape your identity. Your worth is never wrapped in your project. Ever.

4. Your Enemy Will Use Division

If the enemy can't destroy you, he'll divide you. He'll pit you against those people that you have called brother, sister, mother, father, and best friend. He'll place a divide in your home, church, business, ministry, or all of the above.

That's what was happening with the wall builders. After experiencing the extreme persecution from the outside in, now they began seeing division from the inside out. That's the natural progression of opposition. Once we feel the external weight of pressures and persecution, we start to take it out on those closest to us. Sometimes we don't even realize that we're doing it. The

If the enemy can't destroy you, he'll divide you.

pressure inside us slips out with every word and action like pockets of hot steam, burning those we care about.

After so much external opposition, the wall builders' internal pressure cookers exploded, spraying each other with burning words, some stringy roast lamb, and a few figs. It got a little sticky for a while. In fact, the opposition was so fierce that in Nehemiah 5:1, the text states, "There was a great outcry of the people and their wives against their Jewish brethren." Even the wives—who were usually quiet—were barking out complaints. Oh boy.

The people building the wall faced four immediate problems:

a. There was a food shortage.

They were working so hard and yet starving. They cried out to Nehemiah in desperation:

"We, our sons, and our daughters are many; therefore let us get grain, that we may eat and live." (5:2)

Can you imagine how hungry that they must have been? They thought they were going to die if they didn't have food. I'm sure their stomachs had bloated. They were weak. They were irritable. Why were they without food? Because the work on the wall prevented them from working on the farm, thus causing a severe famine. Ugh.

b. Some had to mortgage their homes.

In order to get food, some had to mortgage their homes. These people had to make a last ditch effort to save the very thing they were trying to preserve. You can imagine how tense the situation must have been for everyone involved. They had wrapped their entire lives around this Divine Disturbance. If God didn't come through, *they* were through.

> **They had wrapped their entire lives around this Divine Disturbance. If God didn't come through, *they* were through.**

c. Some had to borrow money.

Others, not wanting to mortgage their homes, had to borrow money from their fellow Jewish brothers to pay property taxes. And their own brethren exacted exorbitant amounts of interest for the loans.

As I'm writing this, I'm saying in my mind, "C'mon man!" Their "brothers" took advantage of a survival situation merely to make another buck. Disgusting.

d. Some sold their children to pay for their loans.

To make things worse, no one had invented bankruptcy protections yet. To pay their creditors, many had to resort to selling their children into slavery.

This became the tipping point. They'd had enough. They were going to quit. This "dream" of Nehemiah had gone too far.

As you can imagine, serious division arose among the people. They were taking advantage of each other. They were selfish. They didn't give each other the benefit of the doubt. And they played right into the hands of their enemy—Satan.

When you're building your wall, fulfilling your Divine Disturbance, the enemy will try to divide your home, your team, your life so you will throw in the towel, lie down, die while the music is still in you.

Are you given to division? Do you secretly get excited when others close to you fail? Or, even worse, are you part of sabotaging their success?

When you're building your wall, fulfilling your Divine Disturbance, the enemy will try to divide your home, your team, your life so you will throw in the towel, lie down, die while the music is still in you.

Do you know Jesus prayed for you about this enemy tactic? Before he left this world, he dropped a prayer in the prayer box that still excites me. As you read this prayer that follows, focus on his emphasis: unity. I think Jesus knew that, if left to ourselves, we would glide towards the divide.

> "I do not pray for these alone, but also for those who will believe in Me through their word; that they all may be one, as You, Father, are in Me, and I in You; that they also may be one in Us, that the world may believe that You sent Me. And the glory which You

gave Me I have given them, that they may be one just as We are one: I in them, and You in Me; that they may be made perfect in one, and that the world may know that You have sent Me, and have loved them as You have loved Me." (John 17:20–23)

So, if there is division among your team—even an ounce of division—snuff it out immediately. Do whatever it takes to create harmony. And not artificial "harmony" that comes when everyone merely agrees to get moving forward. I'm talking about raw, hard, heated, uncomfortable conversations where you hash things out. You

> **Do whatever it takes to create harmony. . . . You might need to go elephant hunting to make this happen.**

might need to go elephant hunting to make this happen. Seek out the massive, hairy elephant in the room that no one is talking about but everyone is aware of, and kill it on the table.

Or, if the Divine Disturbance in your soul is not worth fighting for, then just let the enemy continue to divide. It's okay. He's been doing it for years. What's one more victim?

5. Your Enemy Will Use Distraction

We live in a world filled with distraction. For instance, my two girls, even at five and seven, will watch a movie on TV, listen to their iPods, *and* play a game on the iPad. Seriously? To them it's nothing. (Hey, no jabs at my parenting here either. Maybe they were watching *The Bible* on TV, listening to worship music on the iPod, and doing a math game on the iPad. Yeah, right.)

Hopefully, your Divine Disturbance is building momentum. Good things are starting to happen. Opportunities are opening up. If you have successfully navigated this far, there's a good chance that your prayer requests involve questions not about choices bad and good, but about choices better and best. If you're not careful, you can inadvertently allow the "good" to rob you of the "best" for your life and DREAM.

One of my favorite, often-overlooked passages of Scripture is the beginning of Nehemiah 6. Nehemiah had almost finished the wall. There were just a few more details to finalize. His enemies were at their wit's end at the thought of this guy coming in and rebuilding the wall of Jerusalem. So, the men trying to stop the progress wisely shifted their focus from attacking the *builders* and zeroed their target finders on the *boss*. They decided to make a last ditch effort to distract Nehemiah personally with a "meeting."

> Now it happened when Sanballat, Tobiah, Geshem the Arab, and the rest of our enemies heard that I had rebuilt the wall, and that there were no breaks left in it (though at that time I had not hung the doors in the gates), that Sanballat and Geshem sent to me, saying, "Come, let us meet together among the villages in the plain of Ono." But they thought to do me harm. (6:1–2)

Imagine this picture. Nehemiah was literally on top of the wall, putting on its final touches. He knew that he only had a few more days left and the entire thing was going to be finished. The momentum was up and to the right. The excitement was palatable. The hundreds of builders sensed they were in the red zone. It was first and goal from the eight. All they had to do is punch it in.

Amidst the success, Nehemiah got an invitation to an "important" meeting with his enemies. He didn't know what it was about. For all he knew, they wanted to set up a peace agreement. Regardless of their intent, however, Nehemiah had his mind made up. He was determined. He was not going to let any "good" opportunity rob him of the "great" that he was working on.

Here's how he responded:

> So I sent messengers to them, saying, "I am doing a great work, so that I cannot come down. Why should the work cease while I leave it and go down to you?" (3)

"I am doing a great work, so that I cannot come down!" The work that you are doing, building your wall, living out your Divine Disturbance, is a *great work*. It is a calling. A passion. A once-in-a-lifetime opportunity. So why let "good" opportunities derail it so you never reach the "great" that lies ahead?

As I have been writing this book, I've made several tough calls to say no to good opportunities so that I could focus on the "great" of finishing the manuscript. In fact, refusing one opportunity

> He was not going to let any "good" opportunity rob him of the "great" that he was working on.

nearly killed me. Financially—at least for the immediate present—it would have been a slam-dunk. But it didn't align directly with my Divine Disturbance. After long conversations with my wife, we decided to politely turn it down. Why? "I am doing a great work, so that I cannot come down!"

Here's the cool thing. A few weeks after we made that tough call, the Kansas City Chiefs phoned and asked if I could be their team chaplain! How cool is that? Now, I get to pour into the players, coaches, and staff on a weekly basis.

Because I said "no" to the *good* offer, I was in a position to say "yes" to the *great* offer. In thinking back, if I had said "yes" to the *good* offer, I would not have been in a position to say "yes" to the *great*, the one that lined up with my DREAM.

Think with me here. If you have a Divine Disturbance over the condition of your marriage or family, will adding that extra night of "good" booster club meetings help or hurt? Some of you have let the "good" of social media distract you from the "great" of actually working on your calling. You're more concerned about what so-and-so is doing than focused on what God wants you to do.

I've talked to several people who have sacrificed their DREAMS on the altar of making money. They say things like, "I know that God has called me to be a pastor, but I need to spend ten years in the marketplace first, so that my family can be supported when I make the leap into the ministry." What happens? They lose their passion, and the ministry becomes a distant afterthought. The enemy successfully calls them off the wall. The sundial retreats to the shade.

This move is so subtle that we almost miss it. Don't think that just because you're not offered a good job at the expense of a great one, that this doesn't apply to you. We are faced with the good-verses-great dilemma every second of every day. We don't become masters of the big decisions until we become disciplined at making the small ones. For instance, as I typed that last sentence, I got a text to go to lunch with a friend that I haven't seen in several months. Everything inside of me wanted to say yes. But I knew if I did, my entire afternoon would have been hijacked by the *good*, and this chapter would remain unfinished.

> **We don't become masters of the big decisions until we become disciplined at making the small ones.**

"I'm doing a great work so that I cannot come down."

6. Your Enemy Will Use Temptation

A few years ago in the town of Chillicothe, Ohio, an eight-year-old boy woke up early one Saturday morning, grabbed his fishing pole and tackle box, hopped on his bicycle, and went fishing in the Scioto River.

On the way to his fishing spot, he stopped and bought some worms at the local gas station to use as bait. He fished all morning and was having a great time. By about 11:00 a.m., the worms he had bought had run out, and, not having any money to go get more, he decided to look around the riverbanks to see if he could find any there.

To his surprise, he found a whole community of worms just a few yards from his fishing spot. He noticed that these worms were a bit different than the other worms he had purchased. But he shrugged it off, telling himself, "Well, these aren't the *professional* worms like the store has! These are just regular worms."

So, he spent a few more hours fishing with these new worms. He started noticing that his hands had begun swelling and he was having a difficult time breathing. He decided to call it a day's work, ride his bike home, and tell his mom.

When he got home, he showed his mom his wrists and forearms. He also told her about the worms he found. She noticed that her baby boy was wheezing with every breath. Her motherly instincts flared, and she immediately took him to hospital.

Three hours later the boy died.

This devastation shocked the entire town. The cause of death they found startled them even more. They went back and investigated the boy's fishing spot. They observed his footprints next to several hundred worms. But, taking a closer look at these worms, they discovered they were not worms at all. They were baby copperhead snakes.

The coroner's report came back and said that because of the size of the copperheads, one bite wouldn't have killed him. Two bites wouldn't have killed him. But over the course of the afternoon, the boy accumulated thousands of little bites.

Satan works like those copperhead bites. He says, "Do what you want—one time won't hurt you. It's not that bad." But one time after one time after one time eventually leads to death.

Satan knows that if you see a full-grown copperhead snake, you will immediately back away. Why? Because you see the danger ahead and think to yourself, "If I go any further, I might get bit and die." But baby copperheads look innocent. Satan's has had millennia to perfect his craft—his temptations often look innocent too. Let me give you a fact: ten out of ten baby copperheads grow up to be big copperheads—unless they are killed.

Mountains of books have been written on temptation and how to overcome it. I would suggest reading them all. Multiple times.

We are told that "Satan himself masquerades as an angel of light" (2 Corinthians 11:14; NIV). Therefore, we must know the "schemes" of our enemy (2:11; NIV) and "put on the whole armor of God, so that [we] may be able to stand against the wiles of the devil" (Ephesians 6:11).

The reason why the Scriptures are so clear on this topic is because we have an enemy who hates us. Hates our work. And will stop at nothing to derail and destroy us.

The thief, our enemy, wants nothing more than to steal your joy, kill your DREAM, and destroy your reputation so that you end up disqualified and alone.

Jesus describes it this way: "The thief does not come except to steal, and to kill, and to destroy. I have come that they may have life, and that they may have it more abundantly" (John 10:10). The thief, our enemy, wants nothing more than to steal your joy, kill your DREAM, and destroy your reputation so that you end up disqualified and alone.

When I first became a Christian, my mentor had me write the following sentence on the front cover of my Bible. I've never forgotten it. I pray that you will do the same:

> **"Sin will take you further than you wanted to go,**
> **keep you longer than you wanted to stay,**
> **and cost you more than you wanted to pay."**

THE CYCLE OF SIN

Sin has a deadly cycle. Sin has a destructive cycle. Sin's cycle is preventable! Preventing this cycle is so important to accomplishing your Divine Disturbance, that we are going to break from Nehemiah's story for a moment to learn how. Once you learn the cycle, and teach it to others, your victories will multiply.

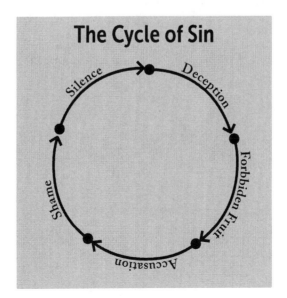

1. Deception

Satan is a master deceiver. He makes empty promises. He writes you checks with insufficient funds to pay them. He deceives you with:

"Come on, no one will ever find out."

"It's only this one time."

"Your spouse doesn't fulfill you. This other person does."

"What happens in Vegas, stays in Vegas."

"You need this."

"You want this."

"You deserve this."

Deception like this has been around since the Garden of Eden. When the serpent tempted Eve with questions and cast doubt in her mind about God's goodness, she chose to take one step away from God and one step closer to temptation. Her reasoning?

> When the woman saw that the fruit of the tree
> was good for food and pleasing to the eye, and also
> desirable for gaining wisdom, she took some and ate it.
> (Genesis 3:6; NIV)

Satan had convinced her that it was "good" for food, and he made it look so "pleasing to the eye." On top of that, he had convinced her that it was going to increase her "wisdom." All of those seemed like really good reasons. Deception at its finest.

2. Forbidden Fruit

Eve took the fruit and ate it and also gave it to Adam, so he could sin along with her. I'm sure this was the best tasting fruit ever. The juices ran down their chins. As they chewed, they enjoyed. That's what sin does. It's enjoyable, for a season. Hebrews 11:24 calls this the "passing pleasures of sin." I'm not going to lie. Sin is fun. But it comes at a price.

The grace period between sin and consequence is pleasure.

That's where Adam and Eve were. They experienced the momentary pleasures of sin. But it quickly turned, as it always does.

> **The grace period between sin and consequence is pleasure.**

3. Accusation

"How could you?"

"How dare you?"

"You call yourself a *Christian?*"

"You call yourself a Christian *leader?*"

"You're nothing but a fake!"

"How could you do such a thing and shame your family like that?"

See the switch? Satan, not only is called the deceiver, but he's also the "accuser of the brethren" (Revelation 12:11). He lives for these moments when he gets to turn on you and throw what you just did in your face. Classic bait and switch.

"You need this...You deserve this...You can't live without it... How could you?...How dare you?...Shame on you!"

In the Adam and Eve account, we see this switch happen as their "eyes were opened." They finally saw the effects of their sin. They heard the accusations in their head—and the accusations led to the next stage...

4. Shame

Shame and guilt are first cousins, but they're different.

Guilt is directed to what you *did*. Shame is directed to who you *are*.

Adam and Eve were embarrassed, afraid, and filled with shame. So what did they do? They tried to make artificial coverings out of sticks and leaves so that they would not see each other's nakedness (Genesis 3:7). They put on masks and pretended that they were okay.

Have you ever considered that the reason you wear so many masks and maintain a false image might be because want to hide your shame?

The natural byproduct of shame is...

5. Silence

Satan has us right where he wants us. Silent. We are embarrassed. Ashamed. Afraid. We don't *dare* share what's going on in our hearts, in our homes. "People wouldn't understand. God certainly wouldn't accept me anymore," we think.

So we hide. We hide from God (or try to). We hide from others. We hide from our real selves:

> And they heard the sound of the Lord God walking in the garden in the cool of the day, and Adam and his wife hid themselves from the presence of the Lord God among the trees of the garden.
> Then the Lord God called to Adam and said to him, "Where are you?"
> So he said, "I heard Your voice in the garden, and I was afraid because I was naked; and I hid myself." (3:8–10)

This is the cycle of sin.

Round and round we go. Will it stop? No one knows. But one thing is certain. If you are going to fulfill your DREAM, you have to get off this cycle.

The greatest part of the story of Adam and Eve is what God does next. After our heavenly Father gives a good 'ol fashioned scolding to our first parents and Satan, he then fixes what Adam and Eve tried to do.

The clothes the couple made out of sticks and leaves to cover themselves had two problems: 1) they were extremely itchy, and 2) they were not very durable. They were artificial coverings. But look how God solved the problem:

> Also for Adam and his wife the Lord God made
> tunics of skin, and clothed them. (3:21)

Most of us read right past that part without giving it a second thought. But did you realize that this was the first sacrifice made in the Bible? Because of the sins of our first parents, and to cover their sin and shame, God killed an innocent animal, probably a lamb, so that they would not live in disgrace. God had to shed the blood of the innocent to cover the shame of the guilty.

Because of the sins of our first parents, and to cover their sin and shame, God killed an innocent animal, probably a lamb, so that they would not live in disgrace.

And so if you're wondering how to get off the sin cycle once and for all, allow the sacrifice of Jesus Christ, the Lamb of God, to be your covering. He will cover you with his grace, mercy, forgiveness, and redemption. Let his love fill you up so that you can serve him for your generation and spend eternity with him.

MAKING IT REAL:

- Looking back at the six ways the enemy tries to derail your Divine Disturbance, with which ones do you struggle the most? Explain.

- Nehemiah chose to avoid letting the *good* opportunities get in the way of the *great* thing God was doing through him. Do you have examples of the *good* derailing the *great*? How did the section on distractions affect you?

- The cycle of sin, as seen in the section on temptation, is real for *everyone*. Make a commitment to teach this sin-cycle principle to someone in the next few days. You'll find the more you teach it, the more the lessons permanently etch into your brain. This is a great way to move these principles from theory to practice. Whom are you going to teach this to? _____

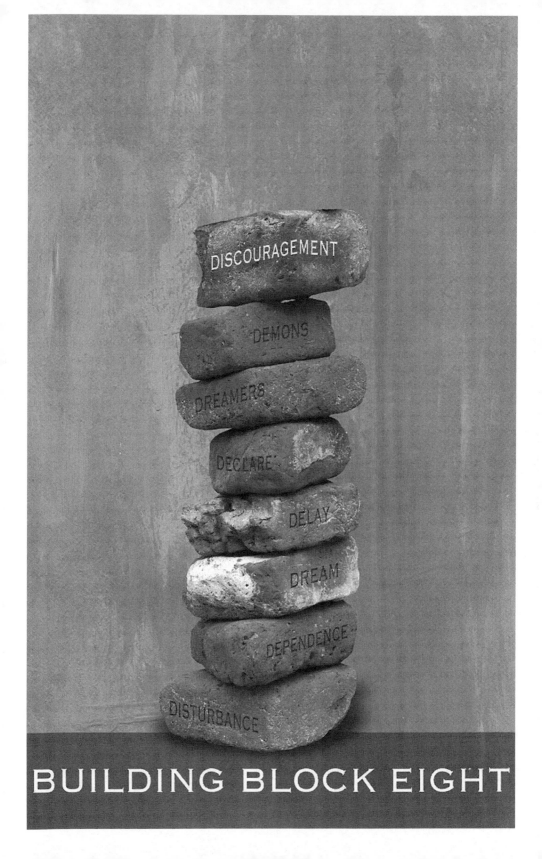

BUILDING BLOCK EIGHT

Building Block 8:

DISCOURAGEMENT

If the enemy can't defeat you, he'll discourage you.

Hello, I'm Phillip Kelley, and I'm a recovering fetal-positioned leader.

Whew. Glad that's out there.

Let me give you some context. Shortly after blowing out sixteen candles, I surrendered my life to Christ. In all honesty, I chased a skirt into church. She wouldn't date me unless I went to church with her. So, naturally, I skipped my hormone-saturated, teenage self into church. And I met Jesus.

Now, I didn't just casually meet Jesus. I *met* him. He met me. Broke me. He disturbed me of my sin and set a new trajectory on my life. I was ruined. Undone. Yet, I was more alive in those early moments than I had ever been.

I immediately went back to my high school and started telling all of my jock friends about Jesus. Now, being the quarterback, shortstop, and point guard helped invoke some influence with both students and faculty. I started a Bible study and saw 156 students come to Christ in just a few months. It was a revival. It was amazing!

My junior year, I had the opportunity to practice with the Kansas City Royals baseball team during their off season. I got released early from school every day for a semester so I could work out with the team. My batting practice partners were Johnny Damon, Jermaine Dye, and Mike Sweeny. Not bad!

I was on the fast-pass to go into the minor leagues and work my way up. But God had different plans.

I decided to go to Liberty University in Lynchburg, Virginia, and take advantage of a full-ride baseball scholarship. Liberty is a Division I university founded in 1971 by Dr. Jerry Falwell, who had an audacious DREAM of raising up a generation of "Champions for Christ." Sign me up!

Yet after just a few months with the team, my soul became *disturbed*. Oh no. Not now. Please, they are paying over $20,000 a year for my schooling. Don't mess this up, Lord.

I had no one to preach them to, just the bags of ramen noodles in my dorm room. But hey, ramen noodles need Jesus too!

Well, he messed it up all right. He placed an insatiable DISTURBANCE in my soul to make a difference nationally for Christ in my generation. Every time I would be on the field taking ground balls, I would catch myself daydreaming about what could and should be. When I should have been focusing on my batting form, I was mentally reciting sermons that I had prepared the night before. I had no one to preach them to, just the bags of ramen noodles in my dorm room. But hey, ramen noodles need Jesus too!

I finally had enough. I had to walk through the Divine Disturbance process. After being DISTURBED of the condition and taking it to the Lord in DEPENDENT prayer for six months, I decided that

I had to DECLARE it to those closest to me. I was going to quit the team and relinquish my scholarship. Easier said than done! But after I vocalized the DREAM that God had birthed in my heart, I knew that it was the right thing.

Most everyone thought I had lost my mind. My parents, who were very supportive of me but even *more* supportive of my scholarship, had to be convinced this decision wasn't a whim. My mentors and coaches shook their heads although they understood the purpose. But my teammates completely understood—because they had seen the whole thing unfold. They heard my sermons in the locker room. They rode with me as I went out door-to-door sharing the gospel to all who were home (and even some who weren't). The one remaining person that I had to convince was Dr. Falwell, the founder and chancellor of the university.

Dr. Falwell ("Doc") was a huge baseball fan. He loved the idea that I was playing for his university and might give them a shot at the College World Series. So when I went in and told him the news, I was a bit afraid. But after I explained it to him, he said in his booming voice, "Phillip, I love baseball but love ministry more. Your decision to quit the team and go full time into ministry is a tough pill to swallow. It's like a brand new Cadillac being driven off a cliff. With my mother-in-law driving!" He always had a way with words.

> Your decision to quit the team and go full time into ministry is a tough pill to swallow. It's like a brand new Cadillac being driven off a cliff. With my mother-in-law driving!
> —Jerry Falwell

For the next six months I was obsessed with seeking God. I got permission to use an empty, abandoned dorm room as my daily prayer closet. Literally, for two- to four-hour chunks, I would lock myself in that room with nothing but my Bible, my journal, and a pen. I would walk back and forth and pray audacious prayers.

"Lord, use me to be your representative for my generation!"

"Lord, I want to make a dent in the world and make *you* famous!"

Ask some of the guys living in dorm 22-1 that year. They can tell you. I was a freshman on a mission.

This DEPENDENT prayer ran through the summer. By the next year (my sophomore year at a whopping nineteen years old), I received a phone call from Liberty's seminary wanting to know if I would be willing to become the pastor of a small rural church about an hour away from school. I assumed they needed a youth pastor. So I said I would go and give it a look.

Well, after driving over the mountain and through the woods (literally), I finally arrived at Sandy Level Baptist Church where I preached my heart out to the thirty people in attendance. Then, after I finished, we enjoyed a potluck that could have fed an Olympic stadium. Now facing a food comma, I was led back into the make-shift conference room (nursery) where the deacons asked, "Well, you wanna be our preacher?"

My inner dialogue went something like this:

> Um, I thought they needed a *youth* pastor. Think… quick!…Are you ready? You're not old enough for this. You've been a Christian for two and a half years. Run. Now!
> Wait. Maybe this is an answer to prayer. You can't change the world staying in your comfort zone…

They probably could hear the conversation going around in my skull, so Roger Stevens, a larger-than-life (figuratively and literally) deacon, grinned and said again, "So, you wanna be our preacher?"

"Sure! Let's do it!" I said.

Then Roger reached behind him, grabbed a stack of mail that said "Pastor" on it and said, "Well, here you go! You've got some catching up to do!"

And that was that. Welcome kid.

I remember driving back to campus that afternoon, calling my mom and telling her, "Momma, you're not gonna believe this, but I'm a senior pastor!"

"You mean a *youth* pastor?"

And thus began my journey of first, explaining to everyone how I got this job and second, figuring out what in the world I was going to do now!

MY DATE WITH DESTINY

Being a nineteen-year-old senior pastor might look glitzy. Trust me, I was also a nineteen-year-old janitor, worship leader, greeter, Sunday school director, lawn mower, bulletin maker, and yes, youth pastor. It wasn't that I was qualified. I was simply available. They were desperate. I said yes. It's as simple and complicated as that.

My passionate naïveté had its advantages. I quickly realized the truth that adults learn on an "as needed" basis. Until we are forced to learn, most of us never take the first step. Thankfully, my philosophy was and still is "Ready, FIRE, Aim." While most people are figuring ways it can't be done, I'm in the shark tank swimming for my life, having a blast, and praying fervently the whole time prayers like, "Lord, if you don't come through, *I'm* through!"

While most people are figuring ways it can't be done, I'm in the shark tank swimming for my life, having a blast, and praying fervently the whole time prayers like, "Lord, if you don't come through, *I'm* through!"

So, I began asking questions to anyone and everyone who had even a glimmer more experience than me. In the words of my good friend Will Mancini, I became a "carnivorous learner." I consumed as much information as I could about what it meant to be in the ministry. And strangely enough, the one who was my biggest mentor through this whole process was Dr. Falwell. Not only had he started the largest Christian university in the world (over ninety thousand resident and online students as of this typing), but he also founded and pastored one of the largest churches in the country—over twenty-three thousand members. I think he knew a thing or two about how to run a church!

I met with Dr. Falwell about once a month for two and a half years either in person or over the phone. Although he had a crazy busy schedule meeting with United States Presidents, speaking on national television shows, raising over four *billion* dollars to build a world-class university and pastor a mega-church, he took quality and non-rushed time to answer my questions like:

- How do I baptize someone?

- How do I preach funerals? Weddings? Communion services?

- How do I run a business meeting? Handle conflict?

- How do I lead leaders who could be my great-grandfathers?

It was priceless. I was a sponge. For some unknown reason, he took a special interest in this baseball player from Kansas who was in way over his head. I will always be eternally grateful.

Well, the church started to grow. And grow. And grow. But I don't think it had anything to do with my preaching or leadership. Those were subpar at best. In fact, I recently dusted off some of those VHS tapes and watched the services. Ouch. I think I need to write them an apology letter. Those sermons were awful!

My first sermon as senior pastor went like this:

1. **God** is with you.
2. God **is** with you.
3. God is **with** you.
4. God is with **you**.

I know. Creative huh?

Our church growth spurt had everything to do with the fact that I convinced what seemed like half of the student population of Liberty to make the hour-long drive each Sunday. I told them that if they came, they would get fed. Not spiritually fed (we know better). But physically fed. And boy did they ever! Our church-growth motto was simple: "If you feed them, they will come!" I had convinced the church ladies that they were helping change the world by making fried chicken, mashed potatoes, green beans, coleslaw, hot dogs, and whatever else you could think of. We worshiped the college student Trinity: starch, sweet tea, and leftovers to take back to the dorm. Hey, whatever works, right? We were experiencing momentum—the place was packed. It was awesome!

> We worshiped the college student Trinity: starch, sweet tea, and leftovers to take back to the dorm.

It was at Sandy Level where I met my bride, Frances. Now, she didn't start off as my bride, of course. She started out as the pastor's girlfriend. Which usually doesn't go over too well (in most states). But when you're a single, twenty-year-old pastor, it's a different story. I was thankful for Frances on two fronts: 1) I had fallen head over heels for this young Puerto Rican with the last name Garcia. 2) The little church ladies stopped trying to hook me up with their nieces named Beulah or grand-daughters named Eunice. And usually the conversation would go something like, "Preacher, my niece is such a great prayer warrior. You two would be great for each other!" Translated: "My niece looks like a Great Dane. She's got a great personality though. Have pity on me and marry her now!"

> **Now, if I'm going to be chancellor one day or lead at such a large level as you do, I'm going to need to learn from you.**

After I popped the question (and she said yes), Frances planned our wedding while I began planning our future. So, unbeknownst to anyone else, I made an appointment with Dr. Falwell, setting up a private meeting that I'll never forget.

Looking back on this event *now* I still shake my head in amazement at the audacity of the twenty-two-year-old kid who decided to take God at his word and live by faith.

I put on my best suit and tie, humbly marched into Dr. Falwell's office, looked him in the eye, and let 'er fly. I said:

> Dr. Falwell, as you know, God has some big things for my life. You have taught me to have a vision. I believe, to the core of my being, that my vision is to be one of God's representatives for my generation. It's not something that I go around telling everyone, but you understand more than anyone. Also, I love this university, and you're not going to be around forever, you know. I believe that one day I can be the chancellor of this great school and follow in your footsteps.

Now, if I'm going to be chancellor one day or lead at such a large level as you do, I'm going to need to learn from you. I'm going to need to know what makes you tick and how you're wired. I need to know the good, the bad, and the ugly. So I'm asking you to hire me as your Special Assistant. I'll learn. I'll observe. I'll write down everything. I'll be a fly-on-the-wall. I'll help you practically by carrying your bags, and you'll help me by downloading your knowledge and vision into my mind and soul. What do you say?

I'll never forget what happened next. He leaned slowly back in his massive blue leather chair, put his forearm on the armrest and his fingers to his lips, thought for about three seconds, and then:

Well, Phillip, in fifty years I've never had one of those. But we'll do it! Deal. The day that you get back from your honeymoon will be your first day. My wife has been after me for a few months to get someone to drive me around, so I'll get you to pick me up in the mornings and you'll be my driver. We'll get you an office inside of mine and you'll be my assistant. I'll get you a seat by me on the university plane and we'll travel every day, to somewhere important. One day we'll be in the White House with the President, and the next day we'll be in the middle of Mississippi. You can stay as long as you want. You've earned my trust. However, as we travel the country, if a ministry opportunity presents itself along the way, you have my blessing to pursue that too. 'Cause that's where your heart really is, I know.

And that was it. A total of fifteen minutes, maybe.

We prayed together that day. It was something that I'll never forget. He stood up from his desk, placed his larger-than-life hands

on my shoulders, and prayed heaven down on me. I'll never forget
a few of the lines of his prayer: "Father, I pray a double portion of
my spirit onto young Phillip Kelley. I pray the next fifty years of his
ministry would be nothing short of remarkable. Allow him to be
your representative for his generation."

What!? Seriously. I was floored. I still am floored.

But I was made to help people reach their potential, and I was feeling that I was a coiled spring, ready to explode.

He was true to his word. Over the next
couple of years, we crisscrossed the country
together. I quickly became the other staff's
"recreation." These other guys, Dr. Ron
Godwin, Dr. Ed Hindson, Dr. Elmer
Towns, and Duke Westover, had all been
with Doc for several decades. They had put
blood, sweat, tears, and money into making both Liberty University
and Thomas Road Baptist Church what they are today. They were a
brotherhood—a fraternity. Now, enter some young kid into the mix.
This could have either gone really well or really awful. Thankfully
for me, after a few weeks of hazing and becoming the butt of most of
their jokes, I humbly took my spot as the "kid" through whose new
marriage they were trying to live vicariously. I could write an entire
book about our daily lunch conversations. Oh boy. It was hilarious! It
was a blast.

My wife got a job at Liberty's Visitor's Center, so we would
often leave for work together. But our days were very different. Our
evening conversations would often go something like this:

"Honey, how was your day?" I would ask.

"Great. I gave three campus tours today and had a welcome
reception for a new group of students. How was your day?"

"It was good. Our first stop was to the set of CNN *Crossfire* in
Washington DC as Doc co-hosted the show with James Carville.
I scrambled to get his talking points together, of which he politely

gave a cursory look and then used none. Then we flew to Chicago to meet with a business developer to discuss a possible future LU expansion. Finally, we went to the studio and prepped for the Fox News *Hannity & Colmes* show where we had to debate the upcoming election with Al Sharpton in front of millions of viewers."

All in a day's work.

Yet this plush job had its limitations. I was in Susa. I was comfortable. I was exactly where Nehemiah was when he was a cupbearer to the king. I could have stayed there forever and no one would have blinked an eye. But I was made to help people reach their potential, and I was feeling that I was a coiled spring, ready to explode. Yes, I enjoyed meeting celebrities every day and flying around on private jets. But there was a Divine Disturbance welling up inside of my soul that couldn't be extinguished. I *had* to preach. I *had* to help people. Staying in Susa wasn't an option.

So, when an opportunity presented itself to minister in one of the most unreached cities in the country (Austin, TX) to potentially hundreds of thousands of college students and young professionals, I jumped on it! Then after about a three-year stint building a ministry, I was called to a church in central Kentucky as their lead pastor. Little did I know, this position would be God's way of breaking me.

GOD WON'T USE YOU UNTIL HE BREAKS YOU

I've heard it said that God won't use you until he breaks you. Well, if that's the case, I was soon on the fast track for God to use me! Whew. I could write an entire book on what happened internally, externally, and spiritually during my two-and-a-half-year tenure as the lead pastor of a thousand-member church in a town of only twelve thousand. The previous two pastors had run off with their secretaries— one after the other. So, the church had little trust in the *position* of the pastor from the get-go. They hated me. They loved me. And everything in between. I was a twenty-seven-year-old in way over my head. Our board meetings doubled as cage fights, and our budget was a mess. Literally.

I'll never forget my first Monday in my office. I asked to see our budgeted numbers. I wanted to get an assessment of where we were. I knew they had just renovated a seventy-thousand-square-foot building, and it cost them several million dollars. I needed a benchmark.

What I heard next floored me. One of the leaders told me that they really hadn't put together a working budget on a computer.

> **Our board meetings doubled as cage fights, and our budget was a mess. Literally.**

What? Were we living in the 50s? They said they had grown so fast that they couldn't keep up with the finances. What they *did* have were several notebooks (the Walgreens ninety-nine-cent variety) that were torn and tattered and equipped with Wite-Out, pencil marks, coffee stains, and plenty of "Sorry, my bad!" initials over the numbers.

My obvious next question was, "Okay, let me get this straight. *This* is your budget? How in the world were you able to get the multimillion dollar loan for this amazing building?"

With a chuckle and a grin this leader said, "Well, we know the banker. And the banker said that if we got twenty families to co-sign on this building note up to $100,000 each, we could have this loan. So the previous pastor (who was now living with his former secretary) convinced twenty families and got the loan."

Shaking my head in amazement, I said, "So, you're telling me that twenty families *own* the church? Twenty families *own* the pastor?"

Do you ever watch a scary movie and you actually holler at the screen, begging the people *not* to go upstairs? As if they can hear you. Yeah, I was *in* that movie, sprinting upstairs. My mind raced and thought, "Right, I try to tell any of the people in key leadership positions—who have signed their lives away for this church—that they, for whatever reason, need to step out of their positions. Ain't gonna fly pilgrim."

That was day one.

Needless to say, God stretched me and broke me during my tenure there. God had given me a Divine Disturbance for my generation, and it came inches away from being hijacked. I am a people person by nature. Crowds energize me. The larger the crowd, the more jazzed I get. So, you can imagine that when I didn't want to see another human being, something was dreadfully wrong. All I wanted to do was curl up and sleep it off. I was a fetal-positioned leader.

> **Shaking my head in amazement, I said, "So, you're telling me that twenty families *own* the church? Twenty families *own* the pastor?"**

Can you relate? Are you there now? Have you given up on the DREAM of God because you have listened to the DEMONS for too long? Have you become a fetal-positioned leader?

As followers of Christ, we are called to "take every thought captive and make it obedient to Christ" (2 Corinthians 10:5). We are also commissioned to not "be conformed to this world but be transformed" by the renewing of our minds (Romans 12:2). Why do the biblical writers place so much emphasis on our minds? Because they recognize that if we don't win the battle of the mind, then we might as well give up before we start.

NAVIGATING YOUR "MIND-FIELD"

What could possibly be worse than an actual terrorist? A mind terrorist! These crippling, debilitating foes wreak havoc on us and on our DREAMS and prevent us from fulfilling anything glorious for Christ.

I'm so passionate about this because bombs of doubt and DISCOURAGEMENT had exploded in my mind to the point where I was inches away from calling it quits on the ministry— leaving my DREAM an orphan, hoping that someone else "more qualified" would nurture it to maturity. I was in a deep funk. Call it what you wish: discouragement, disillusionment, depression, a consecutive series of really bad days strung together over the course of six months. I was in quicksand. Sinking.

I remember this time as if it were yesterday. Every year our church hosted a huge Fourth of July event on Main Street. After a long parade, thousands of people would funnel into what we called the Family Fun Zone, equipped with every inflatable known to man, free cotton candy, games, prizes, and even a magic show. We packed the people in. Everyone was happy. Except me. I was literally in tears.

I had to park my car strategically behind a building so I could make fifteen-minute bursts back and forth. I hid in my car for those minutes to regroup, get my game face on, cry, breathe, and pray. After that time, I would step out like Clark Kent from a phone booth, put on my "public face," and greet everyone with a smile and a high five. No one knew that on the inside, I was dying. I played the part well.

It was at this point of desperation that I called a professional Christian counselor. Yep, I said it. A Christian leader (a pastor even), who had a deep desire to change the world, went to see a Christian counselor. Throw stones. Call me a sissy. I don't really care—because it changed *my* world.

MY FIRST APPOINTMENT

Sitting in his office with me, with a white-noise machine turned on high so the hallway crowd couldn't hear our conversation, he asked a question that detonated a healing in my soul, and years later I would still be discovering its shrapnel. "What lies are you believing?" he said.

"What?"

"You heard me. What lies are you believing?"

Busted.

I sat there in shock as his question reverberated in my confused head. What I discovered was that this question wasn't just a question. Rather it was an invitation—

> An invitation to combat those lies with the Truth.
> An invitation to become the victor instead of the victim.
> An invitation to *dream*. Again.

Answering this question was a turning point.

On a yellow legal pad, I started writing. And writing. And writing. Tear drops started to smear the ink. I couldn't believe it. The things that I was writing were the actual thoughts that had consumed me for twelve months of serving as the pastor of the largest church in that particular city:

"You're worthless."

"You'll never amount to anything."

"You don't have what it takes."

"You're not as good as your predecessor."

"You're a fake. You'll get discovered as being in over your head."

"You can't lead yourself, how can you lead this church?"

"You suck."

"You can't lead. You can't preach. You can't write. You might as well get out of the ministry so someone else more qualified can take your spot."

The left side of the paper filled up quickly because people had told me all these things over the previous few months. And in my naïveté, I believed them.

I had key leaders in our church pull me aside right before I gave the Sunday morning sermon. "Preacher," they said, "we think you're a good guy. We really like you as a person. You're just not a very good preacher and leader!"

Yeah, as I'm walking on stage, this was their encouragement. Awesome.

WHAT "LIES" BENEATH?

On the right column of that tear-soaked paper, my counselor instructed me to write down Truth from God's Word to combat the lies that I believed. In answering his question, I discovered more about God, ministry, marriage, parenting, leadership, and myself than I had in all of my higher education. The subsequent answers to this penetrating question became a rallying cry—a "Remember the Alamo!"— type of experience. I went on a personal and biblical journey to examine those lies I had believed that were preventing me from fulfilling my God-ordained mission. This journey led me to stumble upon a few universal lies that "lie" beneath our façades.

By recognizing these lies, naming them, calling them what they are, and putting them into proper place, we can then go forward to fulfill our Divine Disturbances. If you don't deal with these lies, no matter how grandiose your visions and dreams are, you will, sooner or later, step ignorantly onto a toxic "mind-field" that will send you and your dream into a tailspin of magnificent proportions—maybe never to return again.

> **By recognizing these lies, naming them, calling them what they are, and putting them into proper place, we can then go forward to fulfill our Divine Disturbances.**

TAKE THIS JOB AND SHOVE IT!

That's where we pick up again with Nehemiah. That's where the nation of Israel (called "Judah" at this point) was when they were rebuilding the wall. Passion for this great building project had oozed quickly out of their sweat glands. They were over it. Fed up. To make matters worse, they had listened to their enemies shout mockery upon them day in and day out. Their listening had turned into belief. Soon, they were ready to throw in the towel and vacate their dream.

Nehemiah reports:

> Then Judah said, "The strength of the laborers is failing, and there is so much rubbish that we are not able to build the wall." And our adversaries said, "They will neither know nor see anything, till we come into their midst and kill them and cause the work to cease." So it was, when the Jews who dwelt near them came, that they told us ten times, "From whatever place you turn, they will be upon us." (Nehemiah 4:10–12)

Notice how the laborers now looked at their situation after having endured the crucible of criticism. They had listened to their DEMONS too long. The accusations, questions, humiliation, division, distraction, and temptation became too much. They, who once saw such a great *opportunity* in the rubble, now were looking at the same rubble and saying there was too much *opposition*! The only option was to quit. Give up. Stop. Abandon the dream. Leave it as an orphan for someone else.

The only option was to quit. Give up. Stop. Abandon the dream. Leave it as an orphan for someone else.

Did you also see the exaggeration in the previous text? How many times did their enemies tell them? *Ten* times. I highly doubt that they received the same message ten times. But when we start listening to the lies, one time might *feel* like ten times! Ever been there?

Are you DISCOURAGED? Are you depressed? I think that the first step is to acknowledge that you don't have it all together. Quit faking it. You'll never be able to advance the mission of your Divine Disturbance by masking it. You might fool people for a few months, but it won't last.

Get honest. Write down the lies you are believing. This is not new. We don't need to learn something new here. We need to be reminded of what we already know.

While studying the Scriptures to seek the human lie universals, I discovered that Moses was the perfect case study. Within his Divine Disturbance journey, we see a glimpse of the turmoil within his mind and soul.

Let's take a look at each of them.

1. The Identity Lie – *"Who Am I?"*

Have these questions of doubt ever entered your brain?

- Who is going to listen to me?

- Who am I to lead this project?

- Who is going to read what I have to write?

- I'm nobody.

- I can't compete with the "big boys."

- Who am I to tell *them* how to live when I make poor choices too?

Sound familiar? When confronted with the opportunity to do something daunting, why do we immediately question our identity? This is not a new phenomenon.

Moses was a guy who had destiny written all over him from the moment of his birth. In fact, the Bible says that Moses "was no ordinary child." I'm pretty sure that he was a lizard-looking creature when he was born, just like the rest of us. Yet, he was raised for greatness. He was raised in the palace of the most powerful man in the world—Pharaoh. He was groomed with the best education money could buy. He was given all of the formal training and opportunities of a son of the king. But after running as a fugitive for forty years in the desert, when God was commissioning him through the burning bush experience, he responded with extreme doubt and hesitation.

Remember that delivering God's people from bondage had been a magnificent obsession for Moses ever since he had discovered his true identity forty years prior. One would assume that he would have jumped at this opportunity. But we see quite the opposite. God says to Moses,

> "Come now, therefore, and I will send you to Pharaoh that you may bring My people, the children of Israel, out of Egypt." (Exodus 3:10)

So, here, we have the God of the universe stepping down for a specific mission—an opportunity for Moses to change the world for his generation. What an opportunity! God manifested himself in a miraculous way to offer Moses a chance to partner with him for this amazing moment in history. Yet, look at Moses' response:

> But Moses said to God, "**Who am I** that I should go to Pharaoh, and that I should bring the children of Israel out of Egypt?" (11)

Did you catch that? "Who am I?" Who am I to go before Pharaoh? Who am I to represent my generation? Who am I to take the leadership of this exodus project? Who am I to spark audacious faith?

Sound familiar?

When God gives you an opportunity to be his representative for a specific task or calling, why is it that our first inclination is to respond, "Who am I?"

**If you are going to be used greatly by God,
you must first break through this identity barrier.
It is essential that you understand who you are in Christ.**

Combatting Moses' insecurity, God gave him a paradigm shift response.

> And God said to Moses, "I AM WHO I AM." And He said, "Thus you shall say to the children of Israel, 'I AM has sent me to you.'" (14)

Leverage God's identity for your security. Let his Person consume your thinking. Walk in the confidence that the "I AM" has sent you, called you, commissioned you, and will equip you in your greatest moment of need.

Yeah, but that was for Moses—how can we learn from this in *our* generation?

Here's how you do it. Tweak the "Who am I?" question and turn it into an affirmative reminder: *It's not "Who am I?" but rather "Whose am I?"* Let me write that again in case you skimmed over that last sentence. It's not "Who am I?" but rather "*Whose* am I?"

> **It's not "Who am I?"
> but rather
> "*Whose* am I?"**

This is your permission to change your thinking—now. Go ahead. It's really okay. You might have to look both ways to make sure no one is looking. You're not going to be weird. You are not going to grow a third arm or speak in a different dialect (although Australian might be cool, bloke!)

Is "Who am I?" one of the lies you are believing? You might believe that your *identity* is wrapped up in your ability, age, background, or status. Bull. Your identity is miraculously linked to *whose* you are. You are a child of the King! You are precious to him. That's all that you need to know.

Who am I?	Whose am I?
"I'm just a _____."	"I'm a child of the King!"
"I can't."	"He can!"
"I'm not."	"He is!"
"I am weak."	"He is my strength!"
"I am foolish."	"He is my wisdom!"
"Insecurity rules my life."	"I am secure and confident in Christ!"

Before you go on to the next lie that lies beneath, stop right here and write down what it means for you to move from the "Who am I?" thinking to the "Whose am I?" thinking.

Recently I had two conversations with two different people on two subsequent days who told me the same exact thing. They were *really* struggling. When I pressed them on what was wrong, they finally said, "I feel that I'm invisible. I don't matter. It would be better if I weren't here. I wouldn't be a burden on anyone else. I'm a failure." Two different people in two days saying the same thing. Looks like the enemy has us right where he wants us.

Take some time to do some self-examination. Be serious with this. Don't rush past this in hopes that you'll finish the chapter faster. Pause. Breathe. Reflect on these questions. What lies are you believing? About yourself? About God? About your current situation?

Look at what you wrote down. Now, replace each lie with the Truth of God. For instance, if you wrote *"I am all alone. No one understands me."* The Truth that you can write down could be *"God said he will never leave me or forsake me...He understands when everyone else fails."*

That was fun, huh? When I first did that experiment, it was life changing. That was the first time that I had actually named what was going on. You see, when you are in the quicksand, you perceive reality from the bottom up. You need to see from the top down.

That's why it's critical to take an objective look at your situation and ask yourself the million-dollar question that the counselor posed to me—*What lies are you believing?*

2. The Ability Lie – *"How Can I?"*

Not only do you need to break through the Identity Lie, but you also must address the Ability Lie. With this lie, we transition from making the "Who am I?" excuse to a more formidable foe—**"How can I?"**

If you are going to develop a world-changing mindset, you must alter this way of thinking. Although the Ability Lie is similar to the Identity Lie, it produces a whole new set of reasons why God *can't* do his job through us. If you are like me, you wear God's ear out with these justifications:

- **How can I** do _____? I don't have enough experience, talent, or opportunities.

- **How can I** _____? I don't have the personality, the money, the education, and so on.

- **How can I** change the world? I'm just a _____ (waitress, single mom, factory worker, etc.)

Moses was an excuse maker too. Immediately after God gave him the "I AM" speech, he commissioned Moses to go as his spokesman before Pharaoh. At first, Moses may have thought this an incredible opportunity. But the more he thought about it, the more the mind-fields of doubt invaded:

> Then Moses said to the Lord, "O my Lord, I am not eloquent, neither before nor since You have spoken to Your servant; but I am slow of speech and slow of tongue." (Exodus 4:10)

Moses had a sstt…sttuu…ssstt…stuttering problem. He was not a good communicator. He gave God a genuine excuse. Written down in the biblical text, Moses appears the eloquent speaker he said he was not. In today's language, it might have gone like this:

> Lord, I'm no good at speaking. And I've never been a good speaker. Even after your visitation, I'm still not a good speaker. I am sssssssslow of spppppppeech. I am sss…sss…sslow of ttttttongue."

Before we throw stones at Moses for his knee jerk reaction doubting his ability, we must realize that we do the same thing all the time. When given a task—big or small—our first reaction seems to be, "I can't. I don't have what it takes. I have never been able to, and even with God's help, I still won't be able to."

But if God is going to use you and I to change the world for our generation, we must replace this negative thinking—these lies—with the God's Truth. And in this next dramatic biblical scene, God not so subtly reminds Moses who's in charge:

> So the Lord said to him, "Who has made man's mouth? Or who makes the mute, the deaf, the seeing, or the blind? Have not I, the Lord? Now therefore, go, and I will be with your mouth and teach you what you shall say."
>
> But he said, "O my Lord, **please send by the hand of whomever else You may send**."
>
> So the **anger of the Lord was kindled** against Moses, and He said: "Is not Aaron the Levite your brother? I know that he can speak well. And look, he is also coming out to meet you. When he sees you, he will be glad in his heart. Now you shall speak to him and put the words in his mouth. And I will be with

> your mouth and with his mouth, and I will teach you
> what you shall do. So he shall be your spokesman to
> the people. And he himself shall be as a mouth for
> you, and you shall be to him as God. And you shall
> take this rod in your hand, with which you shall do
> the signs." (4:11–17; my emphasis)

Did you catch how God instructed Moses? God was not surprised at Moses' stuttering problem. The Holy Trinity never went into emergency session because God the Father had apparently made a mistake in his selection of Moses. Nope. He simply said something that is quite often repeated in the Old Testament when people give excuses or criticize. "Who made you, Moses? Who gave you your speech? Who set you up for this stage at such a time as this, Moses?"

Unfortunately, Moses stuck to his guns and refused the role of spokesman as God initially desired. His brother, Aaron stepped into this role. And how did this make God feel?

> And the anger of the Lord was kindled against Moses.
> (14)

Ouch.

I hope that the anger of the Lord is not beginning to kindle against you because of your ability excuses. If those lies are creeping into your mind, put them in their proper place in the name of Jesus! Refuse to let them have power over you any longer!

3. The Availability Lie – *"When Can I?"*

Let's review.

First, we have the *Identity Lie* that says, "Who am I?"

Next, we have the *Ability Lie* that says, "How can I?"

As if these first two lies were not enough, the third and final lie that explodes in our mind-field is the Availability Lie. This lie starts with a simple question: **"When can I?"** But the question is really an excuse, betraying the lies we believe about our availability:

I just don't have time.

I can't fit it all in.

Maybe I need to sit out this season.

Seasons are supposed to change, right? Many people have stayed in the same season of stagnation for the past ten years. I was talking to someone the other day who had been "praying" about getting involved in a specific ministry for twelve years. Wow! Talk about stagnation.

God has given us all the exact same 1,440 minutes per given twenty-four-hour day. The difference between those with a daydream and those who are doers rests in how they use the time their heavenly Father has allotted them.

I believe our availability is one reason why God gave Moses this command in Deuteronomy 6:6–9:

> "And these words which I command you today shall be in your heart. You shall teach them diligently to your children, and shall talk of them when you **sit in your house**, when you **walk by the way**, when you **lie down**, and when you **rise up**. You shall bind them

as a sign on your **hand**, and they shall be as frontlets **between your eyes.** You shall write them on the **doorposts** of your house and on your **gates.**"

Our heavenly Father recognizes that we have a tendency to over-commit, over-schedule, and double-book ourselves into such a hectic pace that we leave no room for doing the *one thing* that God has laid on our hearts to do. That's why God told Moses to instruct the Israelites to **make time.** Leverage the time that you already have to fulfill your God-birthed dream.

Building these times into the rhythm of your day simply means applying the Deuteronomy 6 passage to your unique Divine Disturbance journey.

"When you sit in your home"

Instead of being consumed with the latest television show, how about you use the time that you already have and do something productive. If the Lord has given you a Divine Disturbance for your marriage, do you think it's the best idea to sit like zombies in front of your HDTV motionless and speechless? Or, if your Divine Disturbance includes your children, is a video game the best way to use "when you sit in your home"? Just a thought.

"When you walk by the way"

Unless you live in a crowded metropolitan area, you probably don't do much "walking by the way" anymore. But here in the United States, we do a lot of *driving* by the way. How might you leverage those drive times to process your Divine Disturbance? Let me give you a snapshot of my routine. I seldom listen to the radio in the car. Why? Because I constantly check out audio books from the local library—information that fits what I need to learn rather than what some radio producer chose for the moment—and listen to them while I drive. Why waste an opportunity to grow?

Why waste an opportunity to grow?

Another DISTURBANCE that recently consumed my soul was the glue that bound my kids to their portable devices while we were in the car together. Although I honestly didn't mind the quiet, my soul was stirred at the thought of missing an opportunity to invest in my children. How can I change the world for my generation if I neglect the next? So we started a new rule. No devices in the car (unless they have special permission). We talk. We tell stories. And before I drop them at school every morning, I use the quiet drive time to infuse them with a vision pep talk that goes like this:

> Girls, today is going to be a great day. You're going to change the world today. You're going to help someone today. You're going to use your magnetic personalities to draw people to Jesus. You won't get this day back. So make it a good one!

My girls can almost quote that verbatim. They think it's goofy now. But when they are in high school and college, they will *know* how much their father loves them and is proud of them and expects them to change their world for Christ.

"When you lie down"

Most people wake up disheveled because their bedtime routine is chaotic. Instead of drowning out the day with TV, social media, and other things (which have good uses—in moderation—by the way), how about transitioning your bedtime routine into something that will produce results in the morning? Journal. Pray. Read inspirational material. Talk to your spouse about the day that was and the day that's coming. When you tuck your kids in, motivate them. Inspire them. Pray for them and over them. Don't waste this precious "lie down" time. Leverage it for God's Divine Disturbance in your soul.

"When you rise up"

You're alarm clock is not your enemy. Truly. It's actually your friend. As Zig Ziglar famously said, "Most people call it an alarm clock. I call it an opportunity clock!"[16] Determine to use the quiet early-morning hours to bathe your Divine Disturbance in prayer and to seek the face of your heavenly Father. With a full-time job as a pastor and part-time job as an NFL Chaplain, this book took considerably longer for me to write than I wanted. But I allowed no option of *not writing it* to enter my thoughts. So, what did I do? Got up every morning at four thirty to write a thousand words before breakfast. Call me crazy, but when you're consumed by something that's disturbing you, you'll see what I mean.

> Most people call it an alarm clock. I call it an opportunity clock!
> —Zig Ziglar

You have the time. You prioritize what's most important to you. God wants us to reject the lie that we lack the availability to accomplish his mission. He wants us to prioritize what's important to him, and then accomplish it!

So, the next time the enemy's fiery darts black out the sky over you, you need to combat those lies with God's Truth.

It's not "Who am I?" but rather "Whose I am."

It's not "How can I?" but rather "He made me, therefore I can do all things through Christ."

It's not "When can I?" but rather "I have all the time I need. I just need to leverage it."

INCHES AWAY FROM ABANDONING THE DREAM

You might have had difficulty getting through this chapter because I've been telling your story. You might be where the Israelites were. They were inches away from abandoning the DREAM. They were DISCOURAGED. If it hadn't been for what Nehemiah said next, they would have walked. Is there where you are? If so, I want you to read very carefully what I'm about to tell you.

Hang in there. It will be worth it. God is doing a great work *in* you so that he can do a greater work *through* you. Trust me. I know what you're experiencing. I've lived this mess. It's no fun. It's excruciatingly painful. It's lonely. But the blessings out of the pit of brokenness are unexplainable. Press through. You'll be glad you did.

Making It Real:

- Out of the three lies discussed, which one resonates with you the most during this season? Explain.

- If you haven't taken the time to do the "What lies are you believing/Truth of God" list yet, do that now. When you get that junk out of your head and onto paper, it's amazing how much control it loses.

- Like Moses, what excuses have you been making to God? What, do you feel, is his response?

- Is there someone you know who is DISCOURAGED? Make it a priority to talk to that person and go over this material with them. It will help both of you.

BUILDING BLOCK NINE

Building Block 9:

DETERMINATION

"While women weep as they do now, I'll fight; while little children go hungry as they do now, I'll fight; while men go to prison, in and out, in and out, as they do now, I'll fight; where there is a drunkard left, while there is a poor lost girl on the streets, while there remains one dark soul without the light of God, I'll fight—I'll fight to the very end."
—General William Booth
(founder of the Salvation Army)[17]

One of the greatest movie quotes of all time is from the classic Mel Gibson film, *The Patriot*. America, striving to push open and escape Great Britain's tyrannical jaws, is calling for ordinary men to join the ranks and fight. The recruiters come to the church where Reverend Oliver is pastor, and several of the men from the congregation stand up and agree to join the militia. The scene then shifts to Reverend Oliver mounting a horse along with those men. His congregation responds with distress over their pastor joining the war. But Oliver tells them confidently, "A shepherd must tend his flock. And at times…fight off the wolves."

This chapter is about the fight.

Yet this chapter almost didn't make it into the book. Why? Because the workers of the wall wanted to give up. Hang up their hammers. Quit. They came inches away from abandoning their purpose and leaving the DREAM as an unwanted orphan. The work was too hard. The task too great. They were tired—physically, emotionally, mentally, and spiritually. Harassment suffocated them. DISCOURAGEMENT plagued them. It would just be easier to go back to normalcy. Comfort. Captivity.

Every time he faces difficulties, he prays. Not some religious mumbo-jumbo language either. It's raw. Authentic. Sometimes even vulgar.

I can't blame them. They had mortgaged the farm on this so-called DREAM, and it wasn't paying off. The intensity and the hardship were more than they had bargained for. Perhaps God hadn't meant for them to pursue rebuilding.

Have you been there? Are you there now? Do you know someone who is living the previous paragraphs? Sadly, this philosophy has become commonplace among our generation of "Christian." When things are going well, God is good. When difficulties ensue, it's time to give up.

BATTLE PLAN

Thankfully Nehemiah was cut from a different cloth. "Quit" wasn't in his vocabulary. He was a man possessed with seizing God's dream and seeing it come to fruition. He knew that what they faced were spiritual attacks—and spiritual attacks are best fought on our knees in prayer.

1. Determination to Pray

Although we touched on Nehemiah's dedication to prayer in chapter two on DEPENDENCE, we now see his reliance on prayer consistently fleshed out. Every time he faces difficulties, he prays. Not some religious mumbo-jumbo language either. It's raw. Authentic. Sometimes even vulgar. As you read his honest pleas, you catch a glimpse into this man who had a *Divine* Disturbance. He knew his mission came from God, and God was the only one who would see him through it to the end.

Here are the times when Nehemiah prayed:

1. When he heard the news of Jerusalem, he confessed the nation's sin, reminded God of his covenant, and made a specific request (Nehemiah 1:4–11).

2. While he was having a conversation with the King, Nehemiah placed the results of the situation in God's hands, simply asking for favor (2:4).

3. After being ridiculed and taunted, this former bartender decided to pray boldly for God to do what he wished with his enemies. Nehemiah was honest and raw with his heavenly father (4:4, 5).

4. When the threats and attacks started piling up, he remembered the Lord and made prayer not just *his* priority but *everyone's* priority (4:9).

5. As he responded to the continual onslaught of threats, Nehemiah begged God to strengthen his hands for this great work (6:9).

6. After the wall was built, Nehemiah began to reflect back on the actions of his enemies and reminded God to punish them according to their deeds (13:29).

7. As Nehemiah reflected on his own life and leadership, he continually asked the Lord for favor and blessing (13:14, 22, 31).

Sadly, praying like Nehemiah did is not our usual initial response. We try to fix the bad situation ourselves. We tell everyone else about the situation except the only One who can do anything about it. Nehemiah shows us a better response:

When you're tempted to give up, pray.

When you're back's against the wall, pray.

When the enemy is attacking at an alarming rate, pray.

Pray when you feel like it and pray when you don't. Don't wait for inspiration. Inspiration is for amateurs. Pray continually.

Knowing that backdrop for Nehemiah's DETERMINATION to pray, you might think that he was too "heavenly minded to be any earthy good." Well, quite the contrary. He was fiercely active. You don't resurrect an entire nation without being a man of action. But he was

> **Don't wait for inspiration. Inspiration is for amateurs.**

able to marry his faith *and* deeds together in a way that put him on the short list for a guest appearance in the New Testament book of James (faith and deeds). What we will see in the next section is stuff that would make Hollywood drool.

2. Determination to Fight

The stage is set for failure. The builders are resentful and ready to quit. Dust is their breakfast and rubble is their lunch. Everyone has lost sight of their purpose. Bitterness is starting to spread like a cancer among the builders and leaders. That's when Nehemiah, their leader, stands up and gives one of the greatest speeches of the Bible. He looks into the tired, blood-shot eyes of the men, women, boys, and girls who had, just a few weeks earlier, signed up for this project but are now more DISCOURAGED than ever. Here are his action plan and words that give me chills every time I read them. Place yourself in the story as you read:

> Therefore I positioned men behind the lower parts of the wall, at the openings; and I set the people according to their families, with their swords, their spears, and their bows. And I looked, and arose and said to the nobles, to the leaders, and to the rest of the people, **"Do not be afraid of them. Remember the Lord, great and awesome, and fight for your brethren, your sons, your daughters, your wives, and your houses."** (4:13–14; my emphasis)

Call me dramatic, but when I read this, I picture Mel Gibson, face painted blue, shouting at the top of his lungs, rallying the troops on the front lines of another of his classic films, *Braveheart*.

"DO NOT BE AFRAID OF THEM!"

Nehemiah launched his famous speech addressing the fears that we all face. He recognized that if the builders were consumed with fear, his Divine Disturbance would be thwarted. What fears are preventing you from fulfilling your Divine Disturbance? Fears of failure? Fears of not being good enough? Fears of rejection? Fears of not being able to handle the weight of responsibility? Do not be afraid. The call to "fear not" is mentioned over 365 times in the Bible—enough "fear nots" for every day of the year.

> **Do not be afraid of them. Remember the Lord, great and awesome, and fight for your brethren, your sons, your daughters, your wives, and your houses.**

Everyone has fears. In fact, phobia reference lists record over two thousand specific fears. But I find it interesting that we were born afraid of only two things—falling and loud noises.[18] That's it! We are only born with two fears. We have had to *learn* the other thousands of fears that we struggle with.

And in the same way you learned how to live fearfully, you can unlearn it by the power of Christ!

THE KING OF THE JUNGLE?

When we first got our high definition television, I was hooked on the Discovery Channel—specifically, lion documentaries. I loved watching these huge animals live to the edge as king of the jungle, putting fear into every other animal they came in contact with.

A few facts about the lion:

- They can run up to forty miles per hour.

- They stalk their prey, waiting for just the right time to attack.

- They will attack and kill animals such as buffalo, rhinos, giraffes, zebras, seals, and even elephants!

So, being a fan, I decided to take the family to the local zoo to see this terrifying animal up-close and personal. I was a bit hesitant to bring my two-year-old daughter (at the time) with me but decided that she needed to live on the edge.

After paying our money at the front and walking around observing all of the "lesser" animals like camels and goats and porcupines, I decided to make the trek up to see the King of the Jungle. We had to walk up a dirt path, down a private road, and into the lion cave. The whole time I was talking to my daughter and my wife, informing them all about the lion, how we need to be careful because we are entering *his* domain and all he wants to do is eat you for lunch!

With her eyes wide open my daughter said, "He wants to eat me for lunch?" "Yes, baby. He wants to eat you for lunch!"

With her eyes wide open my daughter said, "He wants to eat me for lunch?"

"Yes, baby. He wants to eat you for lunch!"

My wife elbowed me in the ribs for that one.

Our hearts were pounding out of our chests as we entered the uncharted territory of the lion's natural habitat. I told my family to avoid startling this beast of an animal. But as we slowly approached this monster, everything that I knew about a lion instantly erased. This was no ravenous beast. This was no man-eating giant. This was no King of the Jungle. This was a large kitten. This was the most polite, most well-behaved and civilized creature I had ever seen. Seriously! We spent all this money, made the hike out to this distant cage, and this was all we got—a yawning, bored cat gently drinking water from a bowl and eating freshly prepared meals.

No stalking his prey. No running forty miles an hour. No adventure. No risk. No life.

As we walked back out of the zoo to our car, I had this thought: Why was he so civilized? Why did he seem so bored? What had taken the life out of that lion? The cage. The four walls and ceiling of his new home had taken the lion right out of him. This "King of the Jungle" was now merely a display toy. A domesticated decoration.

I started thinking about my life and the lives of most of my friends who claim to follow Christ. Am I like this lion? Am I full of adventurous potential, full of the possibility to be great, full of power and courage yet caged by my surroundings and satisfied? Am I living my life within the confines of this cage—fearful of what might be beyond the walls?

I love what Mark Batterson, author of *The Wild Goose Chase*, says about this:

> Deep down inside, all of us long for more. Sure, the tamed part of us grows accustomed to the safety of the cage. But the untamed part longs for some danger, some challenge, some adventure. And at some point in our spiritual journey, the safety and predictability of the cage no longer satisfies. We have a primal longing to be uncaged. And the cage opens when we recognize that Jesus didn't die on the cross to keep us safe. Jesus died to make us dangerous.
>
> …When was the last time you asked God to make you dangerous?…
>
> The Danish philosopher and theologian Soren Kierkegaard believed that boredom is the root of all evil. . . . You can't simultaneously live by faith and be bored.[19]

Have you allowed fear to cage you in? Have you allowed fear to tame you and make you civilized, polite, and politically correct? Have you allowed fear to get the best of you and rob you of God's best? Are you, right now, living within the confines of the cage of fear—trying to escape but always to no avail?

If you are in the cage of fear today, I want you to dream with me for a second. What if you were able to escape from that cage, never to return again, and live the life you were born to live? What if you were finally able to conquer your fears and display the godly courage you desire so much? What if you were able to conquer that addiction? Imagine making that move, making that phone call, filling out that application, asking her out, changing your major, quitting that job, taking the job, writing that check, volunteering for that position, taking that leadership opportunity—whatever it is for you—imagine escaping from the cage of fear and courageously entering into the Promised Land that God has in store for you! What a life!

Nehemiah had to convince the discouraged builders of that same idea: do not be afraid.

The main difference between doers and dreamers is *not* that one group lacks fear. Everyone has fears. Without fear, there would be no need for courage. No, the main difference between doers and dreamers is their *response* to their fears. Think of all of the great men and women of the Bible. The underlying theme is not their lack of fear. Rather it is their ability to conquer those fears by shifting the focus away from their fears and toward their great God.

> **At some point in our spiritual journey, the safety and predictability of the cage no longer satisfies. We have a primal longing to be uncaged.**
> **—Mark Batterson**

Joshua — He didn't let his fears cage him in despite his terror of leading God's people into the Promised Land.

Jeremiah — When God gave him the vision and calling, the soon-to-be prophet said, "No, I can't speak, I'm but a child"

(Jeremiah 1:4–10). But he transitioned his fear of speaking into the catalyst that made him a great prophet for God.

Solomon — When Solomon was beginning his rule, he earnestly asked for wisdom, for he said he was but a child and did not know how to carry out his duties (1 Kings 3:5–9). He was extremely fearful but pressed through his fear and escaped from the cage.

Moses — When God called him to rescue the Israelites from Egypt, Moses said, "Who am I that I should go to Pharaoh?" (Exodus 3:11). Again he said, "God, I have never been eloquent...I am slow of speech and tongue" (4:10). But God gave him the strength and courage necessary to be one of the greatest leaders who have ever walked on the earth.

Timothy — God called young Timothy, but he was still a bit reluctant. We see in 1 Timothy 1:3 that Paul, his mentor, had to urge the young pastor to *stay in Ephesus.* Don't give up on these people. Don't run when it gets tough. Stay and bloom where you're planted.

Mary — The blessed mother of Jesus didn't allow her fear of the unknown to forfeit God's ultimate plan to redeem the world.

Esther — She didn't let her fear of responsibility quench her spirit in becoming the queen of Persia and saving the nation of Israel from extinction. Instead of running from her lot in life, Esther embraced it and realized that she was born for "such a time as this" (Esther 4:14).

Peter — Peter was such a scaredy cat that he denied even knowing Jesus three times to people he didn't know! But once he knew how to transition that fear into action, he was able to boldly preach to thousands and be one of the great pillars of the church.

Jesus — Our Savior didn't let his fear of pain and suffering get in the way of redeeming the world by shedding his blood on the cross for you and me.

So, as you place yourself in the story, listen to Nehemiah's words as if they were shouted in your ear. Do not be afraid!

"REMEMBER THE LORD, GREAT AND AWESOME"

When our backs are up against the wall, we are to "remember the Lord, great and awesome!" He's the one who got everyone in this mess, and he's the one who will see everyone through it. When we lose sight of the "Lord, great and awesome," our problems become HUGE and our God becomes small. It's easy to do. I don't blame the builders.

There is power in our memories. Unfortunately, the enemy has taken our memories captive and uses them for *his* kingdom. He holds us hostage by the scars of the past and the wounds of our childhood. Those memories are powerful.

But when we remember the Lord, we flip the script. We recall his faithfulness. We reflect on his perfect timing. We smile at his fulfilled promises. We remember how he delivered us, rescued us, and redeemed us.

> **When we remember the Lord, we flip the script.**

Memory is powerful. My favorite bookshelf in my home office is the one that holds all of my journals dating back to when I was sixteen years old. When I first became a Christ-follower, my mentors encouraged me to record my spiritual journey in a journal. I did. I still do. Everyday.

When I look back at the faithfulness of my heavenly Father, I am engulfed in a sea of confidence for my present circumstances. Remembering God's proven track record will build your faith today. That's why the Bible says, "The Lord will be your confidence" (Proverbs 3:26). We have confidence not in our ability, but God's ability through us, to accomplish his will.

"FIGHT FOR YOUR BRETHREN, YOUR SONS, YOUR DAUGHTERS, YOUR WIVES, AND YOUR HOUSES"

Fight. Fight. Fight. Don't give up. Don't give in. When you feel like quitting, dig in and find your strength in the Lord. Others count on you to fight. Your friends. Your family. Those who will come after you to fill your shoes. Roll your sleeves up and give it everything you got. Leave it all on the field.

As I work with NFL players, I remind the players and coaches often of this quote by legendary coach, Vince Lombardi:

> I firmly believe that any man's finest hours—his
> greatest fulfillment of all that he holds dear—is
> that moment when he has worked his heart out
> in good cause and lies exhausted on the field of
> battle—victorious.

Imagine the day when you are able to lie exhausted on the field of battle—victorious. What will you feel like? Can you taste the sweat? Can you feel your heart beating out of your chest? Can you hear the roar of applause from those you love—those who are on the journey with you?

If God has given you a Divine Disturbance, it is worth the fight. Your family is worth fighting for. Your legacy is worth fighting for. The dream that God has for you is worth fighting for. Don't you dare back down when times are tough. Of course they're tough. All the demons of hell are out to stop you. Intimidate you. Kill you. The resistance is stronger in the fourth quarter than in the first. Fight.

Don't you dare back down when times are tough. Of course they're tough. All the demons of hell are out to stop you. Intimidate you. Kill you. The resistance is stronger in the fourth quarter than in the first. Fight.

FIGHTERS AND BUILDERS

The picture Nehemiah paints next outlines how we should live our daily spiritual lives. We are to fight and build.

> Those who built on the wall, and those who carried
> burdens, loaded themselves so that with **one hand
> they worked at construction, and with the other held
> a weapon.** (Nehemiah 4:17; emphasis added)

With one hand they built the wall. With the other hand they held a weapon. Do you have two hands? How many of those two would you use while building? With one hand they built the wall. With the other hand they held a weapon. Don't rush past this imagery. These inexperienced wall builders (to say the least) were now building with half of their capacity—for a larger purpose. They were wise. They were choosing to be ready to fight. They had a mind to work and a heart to battle. This strategy obviously slowed down progress, but they were ready for an attack at all times.

I want to give you permission to be a fighter and a builder. As you navigate through these ten building blocks, you must have the attitude of both. You can't fight without building and you can't build without fighting. They are two sides of the same coin. Maybe that's why it says in Exodus 15:3 that "the Lord is a warrior; the Lord is His name." Our God is a warrior. He's not going to sit passively by and watch. He's ready for battle. We must be ready too.

Are you going to fight or lay down your sword and let the enemy take full reign over you? Are you going to give up when you are so close? Maybe you have already given up, thrown in the towel, and surrendered. If you have, it's never too late to resurrect that Divine Disturbance and DETERMINE to be broken again so you can rebuild.

Some things we regret doing. Other things we regret *not* doing. Don't let one more day slip away because you are avoiding doing what you were made to do. And once you are building, never stop fighting. Hold the sword of God's Word with one hand and the bricks of God's project with the other. Fight the enemies that will certainly attack, and smile knowing that you're right in the center of God's will.

MAKING IT REAL:

- Think about the reason *why* you need to fight. Finish this sentence: I will fight for my Divine Disturbance because…

- Nehemiah's first message to the builders combatted their fears. What are you afraid of? What does God say about this?

- Building the wall with one hand and holding the weapon in the other is one of the most powerful pictures of spiritual warfare I've ever seen. How does this resonate with you and the journey that you're on?

- Nehemiah told the builders to remember the Lord. Draw a timeline of the Lord's activity in your life. Highlight key moments in your spiritual journey (salvation, answered prayers, etc.). Make note of these and share them with someone else. Then, next time when you're tempted to give up, pull out that piece of paper and remember the Lord.

DESTINY

DETERMINATION

DISCOURAGEMENT

DEMONS

DREAMERS

DECLARE

DELAY

DREAM

DEPENDENCE

DISTURBANCE

BUILDING BLOCK TEN

Building Block 10:

DESTINY

"Every man dies, not every man really lives."
—*William Wallace* (Braveheart)

What began as a DISTURBANCE in the soul of one man finally led to a DESTINY fulfilled. The builders laid the last brick into place a mere fifty-two days from the time they started. The Scriptures record this amazing moment in history very nonchalantly.

> So the wall was finished on the twenty-fifth day of
> Elul, in fifty-two days. And it happened, when all our
> enemies heard of it, and all the nations around us saw
> these things, that they were very disheartened in their
> own eyes; for they perceived that this work was done
> by our God. (Nehemiah 6:15–16)

Fifty-two days! Can you believe that? I can't. In just over a seven-week period, Nehemiah inspired, motivated, encouraged, and organized the rebuilding of Jerusalem's wall. While most of us would have still been "planning," Nehemiah was finishing. And this "finishing" was just the beginning. That's how the final building block works. It might be the final block of a particular step along the way, but it usually doesn't mean you have finished.

It might be the final block of a particular step along the way, but it usually doesn't mean you have finished.

When they completed the wall, spiritual revival ensued. The entire city got together for the first time in anyone's memory, and they publicly read from the Scriptures. When they heard the words of God, the city wept. As if looking at themselves for the first time in a mirror, they suddenly realized how far they had drifted from God's original purpose. These were tears of deep remorse. But their leader stood up and said these powerful words:

"…for this day is holy to our Lord. Do not sorrow, for the joy of the Lord is your strength." (Nehemiah 8:10)

Spiritual revival broke out because of a physical rebuild. Isn't that interesting? Because the people finally felt protected, they were able to sit and listen to the *Word* of God. When they were able to listen, their hearts were stirred. As their hearts were stirred, they turned to God himself.

THERE'S NO REST IN DESTINY

Think of the DESTINY building block more as a large arrow pointing back to the first building block of DISTURBANCE than as a summit or landing point. That's how Nehemiah looked at his role in the story, and that's how we should look at our role as well. Once the wall was built, he began to pray the same audacious prayer that got him into this mess to begin with: "Lord, break my heart for what breaks yours." It's that simple. It's that complicated.

Now that he was praying that prayer, his eyes were once again opened. Now he saw the spiritual and economic decline of the inhabitants of Jerusalem—they were in pitiful condition. So, to make sure that all of his hard work on the wall construction wasn't for naught, Nehemiah became governor of Jerusalem for twelve years and ruled righteously. He instituted a variety of new measures to ensure God's blessing rained on the city once again. The rest of the book of Nehemiah details the governor's highs and lows. Suffice it to say that Nehemiah devoted his life to this legacy.

DESTINY: SOMETHING WE CHOOSE OR SOMETHING CHOSEN UPON US?

When we throw the word *destiny* around, you might sit back and think that this is a passive kind of title bestowed upon a person by the gods. Although the word *destiny* usually means a predetermined lot where one person is inevitably chosen to a particular fate, that's not our definition. Considering the scope of Nehemiah's life, looking back, you can see God's wooing and his setting the stage for an amazing opportunity. Nehemiah just *happened* to be wired with the leadership skills necessary to perform such tasks. He just *happened* to get the job with access to the ear of the only man in the world who could grant him such permissions. He just *happened* to be in the right place at the right time for "such a time as this."

Yes he was.

And so are you.

Think back to some of the experiences that God has allowed you to go through. What has he done? What's your story? Who are the people in your past—both good and bad? What are the influences that have shaped who and where you are today? How has the Lord molded your wiring to bring you to this place? He's been after you for a while, hasn't he? He's been wooing you for greatness since as long as you can remember, but you've been running. You've been scared. You're frightened at the thought of failure. You're frightened at the thought of success.

You've squatted in the shade as a sundial. You've settled into the comfort of Susa. You've lounged under the awning of privacy. But then you started this journey through the book of Nehemiah, and you've unearthed this THING inside of you—this Divine Disturbance—this riot in your soul that you cannot shake. This whole process is just one more way for God to woo you into his plan for your life. Call it good timing. Call it coincidence. Call it whatever you want. I call it DESTINY. I call it God loving you enough to disturb you. To break you. To crush you. And then to build you back up into the person he wants you to become.

> **I call it God loving you enough to disturb you. To break you. To crush you. And then to build you back up into the person he wants you to become.**

Think bigger. The DESTINY that God has for you is way bigger than your lifetime. The ripple effect of a life forged in the crucible of a Divine Disturbance will last for generations. So the question is, what are you going to do with this information? Are you going to remain the same? Or are you going to be a modern day Nehemiah and change the world for *your* generation?

The choice is yours.

Choose to be disturbed.

MAKING IT REAL:

- After you've completed your initial Divine Disturbance, start praying for God to "break your heart for what breaks his" all over again.

- Think beyond the immediate here and now. Think about the long-term impact of your fulfilled Divine Disturbance. Imagine the people you will impact and the stories that will ensue. Use this vision as motivation to keep building. Keep dreaming. Keep being disturbed.

Notes

Endnotes

1. This first deportation from Babylon to Jerusalem was led under the leadership of Zerubabbel and they completed the construction of the temple.

2. Mark Batterson, *The Circle Maker: Praying Circles around Your Biggest Dreams and Greatest Fears* (Grand Rapids: Zondervan, 2011), 13.

3. Hillsong United, "Mighty to Save," (Sydney, Australia: Hillsong Music, 2006).

4. Andy Stanley, *Visioneering: God's Blueprint for Developing and Maintaining Personal Vision* (Sisters, OR: Multnomah, 1999), 17.

5. Marcus Buckingham, *The One Thing You Need to Know about Great Managing, Great Leading and Sustained Individual Success* (New York: Simon and Schuster, 2005), 146.

6. Jerry Falwell and Elmer L. Towns, eds., *Fasting Can Change Your Life* (Ventura, CA: Regal Books, 1998), 37.

7. Gil Bailie, *Violence Unveiled: Humanity at the Crossroads* (New York: Crossroad Publishing, 1995), xv.

8. Charles Swindoll, *Moses: A Man of Selfless Dedication* (Nashville: Word, 1999), 75.

9. W. W. Wiersbe, *Be Determined*, "Be" Commentary Series 26, (Wheaton: Victor Books, 1996).

10. Buckingham, *One Thing You Need to Know*, 146.

11. Andy Stanley, *Visioneering: God's Blueprint for Developing and Maintaining Personal Vision* (Sisters, OR: Multnomah, 1999), 73.

12. Stanley, *Visioneering*, 89.

13. You can find a copy of Dr. King's entire speech at http://www.archives.gov/press/exhibits/dream-speech.pdf.

14. "Jack Phillips (Wireless Officer)," Wikipedia, last modified July 18, 2014, http://en.wikipedia.org/wiki/Jack_Phillips_(wireless_officer).

15. Theodore Roosevelt, Excerpt from "Citizenship in a Republic" (presidential address, Sorbonne, Paris, France, April 23, 1910).

16. Zig Ziglar, *See You at the Top* (Gretna, LA: Pelican Publishing, 2010), 238.

17. Excerpt from General Booth's last speech as quoted in *John C. Maxwell, Winning with People: Discover the People Principles that Work for You Everytime* (Nashville: Nelson Books, 2004), 220.

18. Many popular counselors and fear websites record this fact, often quoting from Ronald Rood, *The Loon in My Bathtub and Other Adventures with Wildlife* (Brattleboro, VT: Stephen Green Press, 1964).

19. Mark Batterson, *Wild Goose Chase: Reclaim the Adventure of Pursuing God* (Colorado Springs: Multnomah, 2008), 6–7.

Divine Disturbance Bonuses

I set out to write this book to be a blessing to those who would read it. Whereas most people charge extra for audio books and other trappings, I wanted to include it in the price of this book—just because! My goal is to write a book every twelve to eighteen months and build a reputation for generosity with all of the material that we produce. So, hopefully, you'll like what you've read or listened to and become a regular.

How to get your bonuses:

Visit the link: PhillipKelley.net/bonuses

Enter password: **broken (all lower case)

(**Please refrain from sharing this link with people unless they have bought the book. My family thanks you.)

The "bonuses" page has every digital version of this book and the audio book (read by the author):

- Audio Version (mp3s of every chapter). This will be in the form of a Dropbox download. All you have to do to get it into your iTunes account is open it in Dropbox on your computer, select the files, and drag them into your iTunes. Or you can play them right from Dropbox. (Playing directly from Dropbox plays individual tracks, not the book straight through.)

- Kindle Version

- Nook Version

- PDF Version

- Bonus pictures and images to download

- If you have any problems downloading, you can contact me anytime at www.phillipkelley.net/contact

My Thanks to You, the Reader

- **I want to thank you (seriously) for reading Divine Disturbance.** The best thing that you can do for me is to live out these ten building blocks. It will transform you from the inside out. Trust me.

- **The second best thing you can do for me is** tell your friends and family about this book or buy them a copy.

- **Also, if you could please leave a review on Amazon, I'd be grateful.** Please be honest. I want others to know if and how this book has changed your life or challenged you in some way.

- **Lastly, I want to hear your story!** My dream is to make an *updated edition* of this book in a few years with *your* stories in it. There's no way I can write the new version without your stories. Let me know how this book has impacted you and how you are living out your Divine Disturbance. You can contact me at PhillipKelley.net/contact.

Acknowledgements

There are so many people that I want to thank for helping make this project come to life:

I want to thank my Mom and Pops for always believing in me and training me up in the way that I should go…My two sisters, Pam and Michelle, for putting up with me and being best friends with your nosey little brother…Kevin Seitzer for leading me to Jesus…Paul Young for investing in me as a high school athlete… Mike Miller for letting me use your lake house to write…Tim Howey and the Grace Church staff for giving me the opportunity to live these building blocks…Kelli Sallman, the world's greatest editor (you deserve a raise…once I sell some books)…My friends who have endured countless napkin conversations these last three years…The Kansas City Chiefs football staff for allowing me to teach through the principles in this book for over ten weeks during the 2013 season…Michael Hildebrand for your amazing graphic ability and wisdom…Michael Hyatt and Andy Traub for giving me permission to actually believe myself to be a writer…The late Jerry Falwell for taking me under your wing and teaching me vision and faith like no one else… Georganna Montgomery for enduring my crazy dreams… Caroline and Madelyn Kelley who are the best daughters anyone could have ever asked for…Frances Kelley who is the love of my life, the one who knows me inside and out, and still loves me…To Jesus Christ who is the true author of life and my salvation.

About the Author

Phillip Kelley is an NFL Chaplain for the Kansas City Chiefs and has been in full-time ministry since he was sixteen years old, becoming a senior pastor at the age of nineteen. In addition to leading five team Bible studies each week for players and football staff, he helps lead a pre-game fan chapel service for all Chiefs tailgaters prior to every noon Chiefs home game at Arrowhead Stadium. He is the co-host for the www.ownit365.com videos that outline all 66 books of the Bible in a creative, one-year Bible reading plan that has over 60,000 subscribers worldwide. Phillip is also a bi-weekly guest on NBC's *Kansas City Live* TV show discussing a variety of topics and bringing a "Pastor" perspective. He and his wife, Frances, reside in a suburb outside of Kansas City with their two daughters, Caroline and Madelyn.

Follow his blog at: www.PhillipKelley.net
Contact Phillip at: www.PhillipKelley.net/contact
Twitter: @philkelley
Facebook: www.facebook.com/PhillipKelleyLive

Invite Phillip Kelley to come and speak at your church, school, corporate event, athletic event, or retreat. He specializes in motivation, leadership, men's conferences, family ministry, and clear gospel presentations. You can reach him at www.PhillipKelley.net/contact.

A closer look...

Frances, Madelyn, Caroline, Phillip

The FCA Faith and Family chapel service at Arrowhead Stadium from 9:30–10:15 am before every Chiefs noon home game. All tailgaters welcome!

Pre-game chapel service for Oklahoma Sooners football team at hotel. This is how a typical chapel looks. Cameras aren't allowed for Chiefs chapel services.

Bi-weekly guest appearances on NBC's *KC Live* discussing topics such as parenting, goal setting, relational issues, and counseling matters.

Daily sticky notes from my girls reminding me to "give me a cac rit naw" (give me cake right now) or "lesgo to disne wrld rit naw" (let's go to Disney World right now).

The printed version of a simple napkin contract between friends at a Mexican restaurant. It changed our lives. Chapter 3 explains.

Made in the USA
Charleston, SC
30 December 2016